TRANSGENERATIONAL INFLUENCE

How to **Live, Lead & Leave** an unforgettable
impact on your generation and the ones to come

Isaac Oyedepo & Samuel Ekundayo

Transgenerational Influence
© Isaac Oyedepo and Samuel Ekundayo 2023

DEDICATION

We dedicate this book to young men and women in our generation and the ones to come. We see a burning generation, a fearless army ready to take the world by storm, depopulate hell, and populate heaven.

This book was written for you to rise to the call of God on your life and impart your world in a way only God could do, through you, for transgenerational influence beyond your lifetime.

You are the prophecy waiting to happen. You are what the world is waiting for you. The earnest expectation of our generation, and the ones to come, eagerly await your revealing. The time is now to live a life that cannot be forgotten, not by human standards but God's, not for selfish ambition but kingdom expansion and purpose.

We believe in you.

ACKNOWLEDGEMENTS

To the Giver of life, wisdom, and inspiration, God Almighty. This work would not have been possible without your grace, mercy, and favor over our lives. We acknowledge the support of our families, our able wives, and amiable children. Thank you for always being there for us. We are grateful.

We also appreciate our biological – Bishop David Oyedepo & Pastor (Mrs) Faith Oyedepo, and Pastor (Dr) J M O Ekundayo & Pastor (Mrs) Mary Anike Ekundayo – and spiritual parents who consistently pour into us and help us mature into who God has created us to be. We are deeply grateful.

We appreciate the great team that worked with us to make this book a reality. Thank you to our Editor, Pastor Sam Adetiran, for your phenomenal work. Our able publisher, Mr Opeoluwa Adebakin of Royal Diadem Publishing Company in Nigeria, thank you for your diligence and hard work. We also want to appreciate RAGE Media Group for the cover design and interior pages layout, Emmanuel Gbogwu who transcribed some parts of this work, thank you for your amazing heart and attitude. To our mentees who served in one capacity or the other to see this work come to fruition, we are grateful. This would never have been possible without your sacrifices.

INTRODUCTION

What is Influence?

Influence is the capacity to cause people to make a change in their lives without coercion. The Merriam-Webster Dictionary defines influence as *"the power or capacity of causing change or an effect in indirect or intangible ways. The act or power of producing an effect without apparent exertion of force or direct exercise of command."*

This means that if we say that someone has influence, it means that they have the capacity to produce an effect in someone's life without force or direct command. If you believe you have influence, the question you should be asking yourself is who is in my life that is making changes based on my life without me having to tell them to make changes, without me forcing them, without me having to coerce them, without me having to command them to make those changes but because they follow me, they read about me, they know me, and they have something to do with me? For some reason, their lives are changing and I am not telling them to make these changes.

That is why I believe very strongly that the world is being ruled by dead men. Many people have been dead for a long time yet their influence is still speaking in our lives today. Why? Because there are many people who are dead but we still read their books, and through their books, our lives are being changed every single day. Through their lives, our lives are still being changed. That is what I mean by transgenerational influence.

Transgenerational influence is that same kind of influence that transcends generations. It is the ability to effect change in the lives of people without coercion or command across generations. Jesus died and rose again thousands of years ago, and is in heaven right now but His positive influence on earth at the time He lived is still speaking today. People are still giving their lives to Christ every single minute all over the world. There are many people who, against the dictates of the government in whatever country they live in, are still living through the influence of Jesus in their lives till today. That is a transgenerational influence. People like Mahatma Gandhi, Nelson Mandela, etc. have died long ago but their influence lives on. I remember asking a young man recently about who inspires him the most, and he replied, *"Nelson Mandela"* Then I asked him, *"Why does he inspire you the most?"* and he said, "Because of his fight for freedom. I feel there is something deep within me that is also fighting for the freedom of people." That was what the young man told me and you could see that the influence of Nelson Mandela's fight for freedom before he died influences this young man that is in his thirties and Nelson Mandela has died almost a decade ago. That is

transgenerational influence and that is the kind of influence God wants for every single one of us. God does not want death to be the end of us and our purpose. Death should not be the end of us, death should be the beginning of transgenerational influence and impact.

> *Death should not be the end of us, death should be the beginning of transgenerational influence and impact.*

Are All Influences Transgenerational?

The answer to that is NO. Some influences are not

transgenerational. Some people live their lives in such a way that they influence people when they are alive but the moment they die, everybody forgets them. For instance, some musicians and celebrities are no longer influential even though they were when they were still alive. I was researching into the life of Amy Winehouse for a book that I am working on at the moment and I read about how Amy Winehouse, who as a young musician was gifted, could hold the note of music and sing in a dynamic unique way than anyone else when she was alive, got addicted to drugs and alcohol. History speaks of how she would get booked on tours and she would not be able to perform because she was extremely drunk and would have to be pulled out of the stage. That influence was on when she was alive, many young girls wanted to be like her but because of her profane lifestyle and addiction, that influence didn't last beyond her lifetime. She died, and today nobody wants to be like Amy Winehouse because of the way she lived her life.

This is why I believe that not all influence is transgenerational. I, however, have to bring to mind that it is not the big things we do that make us influential. Sometimes, it could be the things that are so little and people may not actually believe in them. I am reminded of the story of the woman in the Bible that had an alabaster box of oil that she broke and poured at the feet of Jesus, after which she used her hair to wipe the oil and worship Jesus with it. The moment she was done, it was very clear that Jesus was very excited about what she did and Jesus said that what this woman had done would never be erased from history. That is a transgenerational influence. Jesus said the little thing she did will be remembered throughout history.

Fame Versus Influence Or Popularity Versus Posterity

Fame is not the same thing as influence. We live in a world where people think that both of them are similar but, no, they are not similar at all. Fame dies like a flame. If you are famous but not influential, it is only a matter of time before that fame dies off like flame. Just like the story of Amy Winehouse, Whitney Houston, these people were famous when they were alive but as soon as they died their influence disappeared. That is what fame is like, fame dies just like a flame but influence lives on beyond the influencer. God wants us to be influential not just famous, not just popular among people.

Jesus was very careful to be popular among people. There was a time when they wanted to make Jesus king because he had just fed 5,000 men excluding women and children. So they planned to make Jesus king so He could continue feeding them. The Bible says that Jesus knew that their heart was not right so He removed Himself from their plans because Jesus was more concerned about posterity than popularity. Another instance where Jesus showed that he was not for fame but influence was in choosing His 12 disciples who He poured himself into and ensured that they became who God wanted them to be.

> **If you are famous but not influential, it is only a matter of time before that fame dies off like flame.**

Jesus was building a life of posterity for Himself. He was multiplying Himself across the world through these twelve people. We later realized that these 12 people were the ones that multiplied the gospel and message of Jesus all over the world, and billions of people today are saying that they are the followers of Jesus Christ because of the 12 people Jesus poured Himself into who later became transgenerational in their own impact.

If you are reading this book, do not seek fame, seek influence. Seek to effect change in the lives of people without seeking popularity. Seek posterity. Seek the ability to replicate and multiply your influence in the lives of people so that they too may become all that God wants them to be. Seek influence over fame, that's the Kingdom way. Seek posterity over popularity or prosperity, the ordained over the mundane, legacy over prominence.

The Spirit Never Dies : The Three-Fold Nature of Man And What It Means to His Influence.

The body of man can die but the spirit of Man never actually dies. The spirit of man came from God Himself. The Bible says in Genesis 2:7 – *"And the LORD God formed man of the dust of the ground, and breathed into his nostrils the breath of life; and man became a living soul."* The dust of the ground represents the body of man which is subject to decay and deterioration. However, the spirit of man is not subject to decay, the spirit of man is always alive and that is what makes a man a living soul. It is the divine inspiration and impartation of God Himself into the man that makes that man what he is, separate from every other species that exists. Animals do not have a soul and a spirit. They have brains, they have legs, hands, and all other similar features but what separates Homo Sapiens, which is the man species, from every other animal species is the fact that we have a soul.

A soul is the middle layer between our body and our spirit which helps the communication between our spiritual self and our physical self. For those of us who have been reborn and have a relationship with God, the Spirit of God, which is the Holy Spirit, is dwelling in us. This is very significant because the spirit of man never dies. If a man has the right spirit, he will live on even if his body dies. The source of transgenerational influence is heavily dependent on nature and the nurture of the spirit of man. This means that investment in the spirit of man is what backs transgenerational impact and influence. There is only one way to invest in your spirit and that is to take care of your soul, this is why the Bible says, *"what shall it profit a man to gain the whole world and lose his soul."* That is because if a man loses his soul, the man has died. This is so important in this discussion of transgenerational influence so you realize the power of your soul, the value, the worth of your soul, and the potency of your soul in feeding that spirit that would then live on for life. That is the reason why, till today, we are still talking about Jesus as He is still living among us because His spirit never actually died. In some of those things which we are going to talk about later in this book, we can understand how we too can live lives of transgenerational influence like Jesus in such a way that our spirit never dies and communicates generations long after we are gone.

> **The source of transgenerational influence is heavily dependent on nature and the nurture of the spirit of man.**

What Does It Mean to Be Unforgettable?

I often say that if you want to know that you have influence or impact, just wait until you die. What happens is that in a matter of a week, people will cry, they will weep, they eat KFC or whatever it is they served them during your burial ceremony, and in a matter of time, they will forget you. You will be very shocked that even your spouse and children will soon forget you and move on with their lives. But, to be unforgettable is to have influence, to be unforgettable is to impact people, not just for your good or gain but to impact people with your purpose here on earth, with your gifts, and with what people will remember forever. It was Maya Angelou that said, *"People will forget what you said or did, but they will remember how you made them feel"*.

I love the words of John Maxwell when he said, *"People don't want to know how much you know until they know how much you care."* That means that it is what you give to people without a selfish motive, that makes you unforgettable. And that thing can only be your purpose because your purpose was given to you by God. It is the transfer from God's Spirit to your spirit to make you unforgettable in your generation. It is the expression of God and every time you fulfill your purpose God expresses himself through you and people never forget such expression of God.

> *Every time you fulfill your purpose God expresses himself through you and people never forget such expression of God*

CHAPTER ONE

TRANSGENERATIONAL
Influence and your

Throughout this book, we are going to be talking about the various aspects of transgenerational influence and identity is one of them. It is important to realize that it is not just the name that our parents give us that is significant for our influence and impact but the very name God calls us. There is a difference between the name God calls us and the name our parents gave to us, even though many times God will call us by the name our parents gave us, we have seen over and over throughout scriptures that God has a name for us. That is the reason I believe very strongly that there is power in a name, and God would often change people's names because of His purpose for their lives.

What Is In a Name?

Have you ever asked yourself that question, *"What is so significant in a name that God has to change it?"* The dictionary says that *"a name is a word or phrase that constitutes the distinctive designation of a person or thing."* The word designation is more like an origin, where a person belongs. A name is used to identify or designate a person. That's the power of a name. It is the description given to something to identify their reputation, or its source and identity.

This is important to note because it is one thing to live

the name that your parents gave to you and it is another thing to live the name of your source; to live the name of the God that created you and not the parents that gave birth to you. So many people are proud of the name that their parents gave to them or the name of their parents, that they forget that there is a name that God calls them. The Bible says *"for I have called you by name..."* Many times, when God wants to change a man's life, He will first change their name. He will give them a revelation of their unique name that He has given to them and not the name that their parents have given to them. Sometimes, He will first cancel the name of their parents because some of those names have limitations involved with them, and God doesn't want you to be limited by anything talk less of your name, so He changes that name so that you can begin to have a revelation of the plans that He has for you, that are beyond what your parents ever thought about you.

Can you imagine that some parents will name their kids based on the troubles in the family and those kids will live on throughout their lives with that name unless God decides to take over. Such was the case of Jabez in the scriptures. The Bible says that *"Jabez was more honorable than his brothers, but his mother named him sorrow."* He was named Jabez because he was born in sorrow. Many people were named after a particular sorrowful event in their family that no one wants to remember. Yet, someone wants to keep a memory of such and name their kids after it.

I don't know who is reading this book right now, maybe you were named by the story or the history that your parents had while they were giving birth to you, or maybe because you were not planned by your parents so they named you a mistake. For instance, in the part of Nigeria where I come from, some kids are named *Boluwatife*, and that is translated as *"How God wants it"* that is to say we don't want it like that but this is how God wants it. One of my sisters was named that way because my parents didn't plan for her to come but she came anyway. It was more like she isn't what we want but that's how God wants it and that might create a sense or feeling that you are a mistake and that nobody wanted you. It gives you a sense of rejection and this is the power of a name.

But from time to time when God wants to change a man's story, He changes his name and calls him the name He has called the man before the foundations of the earth. God wants you to live by the name He gave you not the name people gave you. People will name you based on some of your failures, your negative experiences, and your inefficiencies. I remember while I was in high school, I was the shortest among all my colleagues then and they called me the shortest man in the world. At that time I would cry, weep, feel dejected and rejected and no one wanted to be my friend until I outgrew that and realized the uniqueness and originality that God has put inside of me. That made me grow out of such nicknames that didn't hold any value.

> **Death should not be the end of us, death should be the beginning of transgenerational influence and impact.**

This is important, God had to help Jabez because Jabez went to God and said, *"Lord, I know this is what my parents named me but I don't want to live by this name"* and the Bible says, *"God answered him and made him more honourable than his brethren."* If you are reading this, God has a name for you that would cause a transgenerational impact in your life and the lives of others.

The Source of Identity

In the last session, I was talking about how the name your parents gave you and the name God gave you are two separate things. The worst way to live life is to live by the identity that men gave you but the best way to live it is to live by the identity God himself gave you before the foundation of the earth. Why? Because the most precise and the most accurate identity that you can ever hold is the identity that God gave you. God is the source of your authenticity, the source of your originality, and uniqueness. Nobody else can name you better than how the person who created you named you.

I remember when I got the first car I bought with my money. I bought it for 700 dollars. That car was so precious to me, it was the first car I would ever buy with my hard-earned money. I named the car "FAITH" because I remember where the car came from. I was in the church at that time, and right where I was that day God told me *"Sam go and wash the toilet."* At that time, I was still studying for my Ph.D., so washing the toilet looked somehow. I was not in the sanctuary keepers department, it was not something I have done within the church environment before. God said, *"Go and wash the toilet"* While I was still ruminating on whether I would or wouldn't, God said, *"If you wash that toilet I will buy you a car."*

Knowing how God speaks to me, I did not doubt that it was God speaking. At that particular point in time, I could never afford the money to buy a car, so I knew that was God. So, I decided instantly to obey. There were two toilets in the church I attended and this was around 2011 or 2012. I remember I got the soap and the brush and washed the toilets properly with my hands from top to bottom. I washed it so well because I knew that was the source of the car that God wanted to give me.

As soon as I was done, I could almost feel the smile of heaven raining down on a son who had just obeyed God. Only about two or three weeks later, my pastor and father in the Lord said, *"Samuel guess what, I just got you a car."* I was like, *"Wow! Got me a car? How?"* He continued, *"I have not paid for it and I don't think I have all the money to pay for it, but someone in my office wanted to sell their precious car."* A lady in her fifties had been using this car since about 1995 and she wanted to let go of it because she wanted to buy a brand new car and because it was so precious, she didn't want to sell it anyhow. She felt like giving it as a gift to someone. My pastor heard about it and was like *"Yes! I need to give it to my son in the Lord. I promise you he will take care of it."* Before my pastor asked how much she was going to sell it for, he secured it for me. By the time we asked the lady how much she was going to sell it for, she said 700 dollars. Everything I had saved up at that time wasn't up to 700 dollars but this woman, because she trusted my pastor, said she was going to keep that car until I could raise the money. I was able to eventually pay that 700 dollars and I got my car with my money. It was amazing and it came out of the fact that God spoke.

I want to let you know that the reason why I treasure that car and gave it a name was because of how it came. God gives us His unique name because of how we came through Him. There is a part of God that you share with Him and that part is so precious that He gave you a name. If you don't know what that name is, I want to implore you to spend some time with God and ask Him, *"What is the name You have given me."* If you find out what that name is, you will find the source of your identity, the source of your uniqueness, and the source of your originality. The best way to live life is to live it originally, not to live it like a photocopy or to live it like you are unfounded and you don't know where you came from.

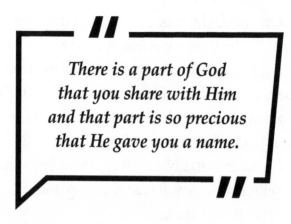

> *There is a part of God*
> *that you share with Him*
> *and that part is so precious*
> *that He gave you a name.*

Your Authenticity, Your Originality, Your Uniqueness.

In this session, I want to talk about how your name, your identity can be the source of your authenticity, originality, and your uniqueness. God is so big, so mighty and so amazing that it is impossible for Him to put His entire self in one man. In one of my books, *Purpose in Crisis*, I shared how God put a dimension of Himself into every man. God gave me a direct revelation from Genesis Chapter 2:7. I finished reading that scripture that day and I started to question God from that scripture that says, *"God breathed into man, and man became a living soul."* I asked God, *"Lord, did you put your entire self into the man?"* Because the phrase *"Breathe into man"* came from the Hebrew word *"Nasham"* and it means *"Divine inspiration, divine impartation."* And God said, *"No, I didn't put my entire self into man, if I put my entire self into man, man would have become GOD and that would be against my nature so what I did was put a part or dimension of myself into each man."*

Because God is so big and wide every one of us can only accommodate a part of God. That means you, who is reading this right now, have a dimension of God inside of you and that is the source of your uniqueness and authenticity. There is something about you that God Himself carries. There is a nature, dimension, or part of God that you carry and that is the source of your uniqueness and authenticity. That is what makes you different from everyone else, it separates you from the pack. It is what makes you unique in your own right that you don't have to copy anybody or compete with anybody.

When you find what that dimension of God is on your inside, you find your authenticity and originality. The point I am trying to make is when you are connected to your source, you find your true identity. You find your name, and often when God renames you based on the dimension of Him in you, He backs it with a statement of how your life would be thereafter. In the latter part of this session, I will share with you some of those people who every single time God reveals that dimension of Himself in them to them, He tells them what it means and as a result, they live lives of transgenerational impact and influence and live in such a way that they never die. Today, we are still talking about so many of them and that is why I am using them as examples in this book.

Some Examples:
Abram Becoming Abraham

Abram means *"father of one"* and when you look at what God wanted to do with Abraham, he could not continue bearing the name Abram because it wouldn't work. God wanted to make Abraham the father of nations. How can the father of nations be the father of one, they don't work together? The dimension of God in Abraham was that he was going to reproduce many nations. He was not just going to reproduce one person. Of course, the situation and circumstance of Abraham at that time was not a father of nations yet, I mean this very Abraham at old age didn't have a son yet and God is saying I will give you the name Abraham because you will be the father of many nations. I don't know who is reading this book right now, your situation and circumstance may look different or not align with what God says He would do through you or the name that God gave to you. Hold on, hold on.

God is intentional in the name that He gives to us. God is very sure, your situation may make you doubt your real identity but hold on to it because God knows what

He is doing. At the end of the day, Abraham eventually had a son and every of God's promises when he told him to count the stars, to count the sand of the seashore, all came to pass through Isaac.

The uniqueness that God has for you is embedded in the name that He has for you. The impact and transgenerational influence God has for you is embedded in the name He has for you. Abraham went on to be the father of many generations and today we still sing that song, *"Abraham's blessings are mine."* The very blessing that God gave Abraham based on the new name He gave to him, we are still claiming it till today. God told him, *"Your seed would be as the stars and no one would be able to number them."* It reminds me of one of the descendants of Abraham, the man called Jacob.

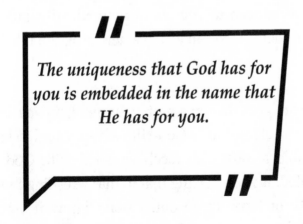

The uniqueness that God has for you is embedded in the name that He has for you.

Jacob Becoming Israel

The name "Jacob" has a lot to do with cheating, swindling people, and Jacob has done this for many years in his life. It got to a point where God said it's about time I took over, it's about time I let you know your identity has nothing to do with swindling people and cheating people, it's about time I reinstall a new program into you. Sometimes, you can be carrying a Trojan virus and never know until an expert comes into the room and says *"We need to clean this computer."* That was the case of Jacob. God said, *"No I did not create this boy to be a cheat."*

If you are reading this book and everything that has been happening in your life is not in sync with everything that has been promised you or everything God has spoken to you about your identity, hold on, hang in there. God can install a new program into your life.

The story goes that on a particular night, an angel who was later referred to as God Himself appeared to Jacob. The Bible records that Jacob wrestled with God and prevailed. It was amazing that in that wrestling the real identity of Jacob came out. I don't know if you are reading this and have been wrestling and struggling with God all your life. You are in this dichotomy between the bull and the horn of who you are now and who God has created you to be.

The truth is that wrestling eventually leads to transgenerational impact and influence if you would allow God to have His way. God broke the thigh of Jacob so He could have His way because Jacob was so strong that he wrestled with God and was almost prevailing. He said, *"Lord, I will not let you go until you bless me."* We could see the blessing of a name because the blessing was not just pronounced on Jacob that he was going to have many goats and cattle, the blessing was a change of his name. Someone is reading this book right now, and the blessing that you need is not in some big car, a big house, or an increment of salary but the blessing that you need is a change of name. That change of name reinforces the transgenerational influence that God has in store for you.

As soon as God was done, He said, *"Your name will no longer be Jacob but Israel."* Guess what? That is in line with what God told Abraham, He became the father of Israel and eventually became the father of many nations till today.

Simon Becoming Peter (Cephas).

Just like Jacob, the name Simon didn't sound like the kind of name you will be proud of, it means *"Shaky as a leaf on water, very doubtful and very untrustworthy"*. That was the name of Simon Bar Jonah but there came an encounter in the book of Matthew Chapter 16 that soon changed Simon's life. All his life, Simon had lived up to his name because he had not come to a reality of his true identity. In Matthew 16, Jesus asked the disciples, *"Who do you say I am?"* Some people said Jeremiah, Some said John the Baptist, and everyone had different kinds of suggestions but I saw something so powerful there. Simon said, *"Jesus, you are the Son of God."* Amazing *revelation. Jesus responded and said, "Simon, flesh and blood has not revealed this to you but my father in heaven."*

The meaning of that is that the revelation of who God is is very critical to the revelation of who you are. It was what Jesus said next that we must study. Jesus said, *"You are Simon, but from now on you are a rock (translated as "Cephas") and upon this rock I will build my church and the gate of hell shall not prevail against it."* From that moment on, the very same Peter that was unstable became stable. That same Peter preached in one day and 3000 people were added to the church. That same Peter stood before the leaders of the city and spoke, and they said *"No this man is not educated, how come he is speaking this way?"* It is because the moment his true identity kicked in, transformational impact started. Peter began to do the things that he would not have been able to do ordinarily.

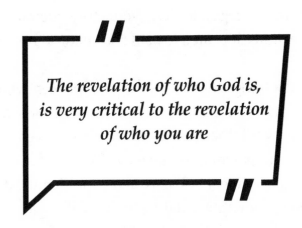

> *The revelation of who God is, is very critical to the revelation of who you are*

I don't know who is reading this book and you have always been doing things as shaky and unstable as Simon before he became Cephas, God is saying to you that in the name He has for you, is where your transgenerational impact and extraordinary influence exists. That was what made Peter the rock that Jesus built his church upon.

Saul Becoming Paul

Saul had been doing some detrimental things to the body of Christ. He had been killing Christians all over from Jerusalem to Judea to Damascus, in fact everywhere. One day he set out to Damascus ready to do what he has always been doing, like a hunter after a game. He was so set on his mission, trying to kill as usual but that day, heaven said no! Enough is enough, you have lived a false identity enough. This time you are going to begin to live your true identity and purpose. Jesus appeared to Saul and changed his name.

One of the things that closes the gap between who we are now and who God wants us to be is our new name and identity. It is the name God himself has given us not the name our parents have given us. That is what I mean by transgenerational influence and your identity. If you get your identity right, you will get your transgenerational influence right because God's name for you is the root and the source of your transgenerational influence. Find out what your God-given name is, seek the Lord in prayer, and say, *"Lord, reveal my real identity to me."*

I remember doing a clarity session for a young man recently and during that clarity session, God ministered to me and said, *"He has a name, I have given him a name. Tell him to go find out that name."* I gave the young man a fast to do and by the time he came back he said *"Yes, sir. I now know the name, the name is the son of encouragement."* We both smiled that day and we soon realized what God had called him to be, to encourage generations and nations. I believe very strongly that if that young man adopts the name and begins to live according to that purpose every single day of his life, he is going to live a life of transgenerational influence. I pray that you reading this book will live such a life in Jesus' name.

> *If you get your identity right, you will get your transgenerational influence right because God's name for you is the root and the source of your transgenerational influence*

My Story

I remember while I was growing up as a teenager, I used to be very stubborn, so stubborn that my parents couldn't control me at that particular point in time. Every single time they asked me not to do something, I would do that very thing the next day. One of the things that was particularly a major headache for my parents was football. They will ask me not to play football especially with a certain set of kids but those were the kids I wanted to play with. Every single day they will punish me and I will still go the next day.

It was as though I was not ready to listen to them at all and I was giving them this tough time. Until one day my mother made a powerful realization and she said that God spoke to her that they should stop calling me one of my names. That name was Ayodeji and Ayodeyi means *"My Joy has multiplied by two"*. My mother's revelation came out of the word "Ayo", Ayo simply means joy or excitement so to speak. But there is a way the Yorubas can translate Ayo to mean excessive, exuberant kind of joy that can make one to be exuberant beyond measure.

So, my mom said that God said they should stop calling me that kind of name and start calling me my other name, "Moyosore" which is my real name. It means, *"I rejoice at the gift"* The name Ayodeji was given to me by one of my grandfathers because he loved me so much and he had a profound influence on my parents, so they adopted the name and were calling me that at that particular point in time.

As soon as my mother got that revelation, she changed my name and something happened in the realm of the spirit that I can't particularly explain. All I knew was that a few weeks after that name change I sat down in my room and without anyone preaching to me, I said to myself enough is enough of all the troubles my parents have had about me, and from that day on I was going to make a change for the better. I made that decision within myself, I didn't tell anyone, I didn't tell my mom or my dad but in reflection, I realize that it was because of that revelation of that name change that God gave my mother. And as a result of that change of identity, it affected how I began to live my life. No one called me Ayodeji again, anyone who did probably knew me back then. All of my family adopted the name Moyosore. That name change birthed the real me that God had in mind from the beginning of time.

The Story of John The Baptist.

The Bible says an angel had appeared to the father of John the Baptist, Zacharias, and told him that He will bear a son named John and declared all the purposes of John. The angel said that name matches with all John is going to do in life. Just like the name Jesus, the Bible says in Matthew 1:21, *"And she will bring forth a Son, and you shall call His name Jesus, for He will save His people from their sins."* That name is significant to the purpose of his life, the same was that of John the Baptist.

The angel gave the name and the purpose behind the name. Something shocking happened at the birth of the child. The family members came to the naming ceremony of John and decided that the child was not going to be named John. Unfortunately, at that time, the father was dumb. The angel had made him dumb for slightly doubting the message God sent and this was because Zechariah and his wife, Elizabeth, had been waiting for a son for ages. Being human, it was easy for him to be doubtful.

So, the family members were mounting pressure on Elizabeth to name the child after his father, Zacharias. Nobody in their family had heard that kind of name, John, before. They wondered where the parents got that name from. They persuaded her to name the boy Zacharias so he can be a priest in the stead of his father. The Bible says *"Elizabeth stood her ground"* and insisted that the child be named John, not Zacharias.

After a lot of disagreement, they had to ask the father of the child what he would like to name the child and Zacharias took a pen and paper and wrote "JOHN" That settled the case completely because someone knew the name that heaven had given the child and knew that the name was significant for his transgenerational impact and influence, hence they did not allow anybody change that name.

I don't know who might be reading this book now and the world has tried to change your name and identity.

They have tried to tell you that the purpose you have is weird, *"Nobody lives life like that anymore."* It is not a tradition or a trend, don't let them change your name, don't let them turn you into who you are not. Who you are is who God wants you to be. The name He has given you is connected to your transgenerational impact and influence. The devil will always try to use people you respect to change it, the devil will try to use your teachers to call you average and mediocre. The devil will use people to call you all sorts of names but you must never let them change your name. If you let them change your name, they will alter your destiny.

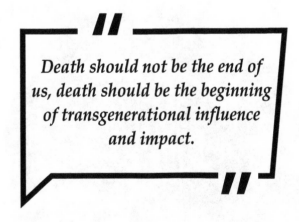

> **Death should not be the end of us, death should be the beginning of transgenerational influence and impact.**

If you don't know that name, find that name. Spend some time with God and say, *"Give me the name that you have named me from the foundations of the earth."* Amen.

CHAPTER TWO

TRANSGENERATIONAL
Influence and
your PURPOSE

What is Purpose?

Purpose is the mind of God about you. It is the mind of the creator about a thing for creating anything. God is the creator and purpose is the mind of God about us. This means that for us to live a life of purpose, then we must know what God has in mind for us. The Bible says, *"Eyes have not seen, ears have not heard neither has it come to the mind of man what God has in mind for those who love Him"* What this means is that nobody knows your purpose, no eyes have seen it, and no mind has conceived it. Even the astrologers who read the stars and the palmist cannot tell you your purpose.

The Bible says even those things will be revealed to us by the Spirit of God. It takes the Spirit of God to reveal your purpose to you because if you get your purpose from anybody else, it would not lead to transgenerational impact and influence. It is only the purpose of God for your life that will lead to transgenerational impact and influence. This is why we must seek to know the mind of God for our lives. The mind of God is not hard to know, all we need to do is seek. Have a relationship with the Holy Spirit and He will reveal the mind of God to you. The scripture says in 1 Corinthians 2:11 *"For what man knows the things of a man, save the spirit of man which is in him? Even so the things of God knows no man, but the Spirit of God"*. If you consult the Spirit of God about you, you will know the mind of God about you.

The source of purpose is not man, the source of purpose is not your parents, the source of purpose is not your government, the source of purpose is not your career, the source of purpose is God Himself because purpose existed way before you were conceived in the womb of your mother. Purpose existed long before your father and mother had anything to do with each other. God had you in mind already even before your parents were born. Before the foundations of the earth, God carried us like babies inside His womb. God was pregnant, thinking about how the world will look like with us inside of Him, He was thinking of our assignments and what He would have us do. What man thinks of you is not your purpose, what man thinks of you has nothing to do with God's purpose for your life. What God thinks of you is what is supreme and primary.

The source of your purpose is not man, the source of your purpose is God Himself. He told Jeremiah in Jeremiah 1:5, *"Before I formed you in the womb I knew you."* What that means is that before your parents decided to do anything together, He knew you. The Bible says in Romans 8:29, "Who God foreknew, He also predestined." In other words, before the very foundations of the earth, God knew us. God set the end even before the beginning. We cannot leave our purpose to man, you cannot allow man to determine your purpose.

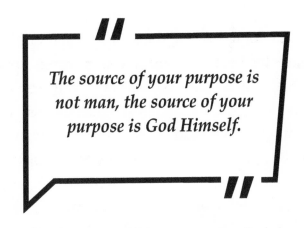

The source of your purpose is not man, the source of your purpose is God Himself.

Our purpose has been decided by God before the foundations of the earth, He is the One that decided who we are and decided what we were going to do. This makes purpose a priority over everything else.

The Power And Priority of Purpose

Life without priority is a misplaced life and a misplaced priority will lead to a misplaced life. It is important to note the things in life that we make a priority. The word priority in the dictionary speaks about the quality or state of being prior, allocating something in the order of importance. This is very powerful because, in God's grand scheme of things, purpose is of great importance.

It is impossible to discover your purpose without having a relationship with God. It was stated earlier that the source of purpose is God. That makes purpose something of a priority.

If you are going to have transgenerational impact and influence, then you must make your purpose a priority. The Bible, in Matthew 6:33, declares, "But seek ye first the kingdom of God, and his righteousness; and all these things shall be added unto you". God wants us to live in such a way that our priority is the kingdom of God. The Kingdom of God speaks of our kingship, our dominion which I am going to talk about in another chapter. But in summary, it speaks about our purpose. Knowing what God has called you to do and seeking it first. Seeking it first means making it a priority, making it the center of your life, pouring your entire life into it and doing that together with righteousness and holiness, and the Bible says that every other thing that you seek will be added to you.

When you make God a priority, everything else will be attracted to you but when you make God last place, everything else will not be attracted to you. When you chase things and leave God, you will lose God and lose things. But when you chase God at the expense of things, you will gain God and still gain those things. That is why the Bible says we should not be afraid of any man who can kill the body only, we should rather be afraid of God who can kill the body and the soul in Hellfire. Purpose is a priority.

> *When you make God a priority, everything else will be attracted to you but when you make God last place, everything else will not be attracted to you.*

I make sure that my priority in life is based on my relationship with God, my purpose, my family, and my love for people. Those are the key things that drive me every single time. Purpose is placed at the top of my priority, every morning I wake up and the question I am asking is *"How do I fulfill purpose today?"* In other words, *"How do I help someone find their purpose today?"* Since I discovered God's purpose for my life, I soon realized that is the priority for my life. In the year 2016, I realized that I have so many gifts and I will be giving account for those gifts later on when I get to see God and that scared me a little bit. I remember I couldn't sleep for a while and I knew that I needed to find God's purpose for my life. I went to God in prayers and after some days, God said to me, *"Your purpose is to help other people discover their purpose."* I wrote that down and I soon made it the priority of my life every single day.

I soon realized that helping people every day to discover their purpose has raised my value and shot up my value and effectiveness in life. People seek after me to help do what God has created me to do in their lives. If you are reading this book right now and you don't know what your purpose is, I want to give you an assignment, and that is to spend some time with God asking God one which is, *"Lord, what is my purpose in life."* That was what I did in 2016 and God spoke to me. You too must do the same because you must make your purpose a priority. If you are going to live a life of transgenerational impact, you cannot live it doing what you are not called to do. You cannot have transgenerational impact and influence doing what you are not called to do, you can only live a life of transgenerational impact doing what you were born and created to do. If there is a misalignment between what you are called to do and what you are doing, then you will never have transgenerational impact and influence. When there is an alignment between what you are called to do and what you are doing, then you will have transgenerational impact and influence.

I always tell people not to live their life doing their own

assignment but to live life doing God's assignment. Everything that you do outside of what you are called to do will make you a failure but when you do what you are called to do, that is when you are a success. Success in the eyes of God is multiplication. To multiply what God has given you, you must impact people with what you have been given. Multiplication is also an influence. When you have influence, God sees you as a successful servant. He called the servants in Mathew 25 who turned five talents to ten, and two to four, *"Thou good and faithful servant."* The Bible says it is required of stewards to be faithful. So, it is important that you find God's purpose for your life and make it a priority.

> *When there is an alignment between what you are called to do and what you are doing, then you will have transgenerational impact and influence*

The Nature of God Is Transgenerational

Everything God does transcends from generation to generation. When God speaks to one man, He is speaking to an entire generation. When God speaks to a nation, He is speaking to generations after them. From time to time, we see in the scriptures that God likes to deal in transgenerational things. The purpose for God in our life is for transgenerational impact. The Bible says He has placed eternity in our hearts. What that means is that every single time we do what God has called us to do, that thing could last for eternity.

Every time you do what you are created to do, you are setting yourself up for transgenerational impact and influence. This means that the nature of God is what is expressing itself through you. Like I said in the earlier chapter if you allow God to express himself through you, what you are doing is setting yourself up for God to have a transgenerational impact through you on the world. That is how God works and we have that nature of God. The Bible tells us that God created us in His likeness and image, which means with His nature and characteristics.

> *Every time you do what you are created to do, you are setting yourself up for transgenerational impact and influence.*

If you have the image and characteristics of God, you are also going to have the transgenerational nature of God. There is only one way to have that transgenerational nature, it is by aligning ourselves with God's purpose. When you live God's purpose for your life, you live a fulfilled life. A fulfilled life is a life that makes God happy, it's a life that pleases God and makes Him smile. When God is pleased, He releases grace for you to do more. That is why after you are long dead and gone, your influence still lives on because you have fulfilled your purpose.

Purpose is an eternal race. When you find your purpose, the rat race will bore you. When you find your purpose, eternal race will be your watchword. You will be always eager to live beyond your lifetime. This is why people who have found their purpose are never afraid to die. That is because they know they cannot die, the smallest part of death is dying in your flesh. The real death is dying in your spirit and your spirit no longer has impact and influence. That is not what God wants for us, God wants us to live such that when we die in our body our spirit lives on impacting generations after us; our books live on, our messages live on. The people our lives have touched and impacted continue to live on and live under that purpose that God has given us.

The Bible talks about the burden that God has placed upon man, it is for eternity. It never ends and you should not let it end by chasing mundane and mere things. A transgenerational impact is what God has for you and he has it rooted and encoded in your purpose that is why you must find your purpose. You must make it a priority by focusing on it and making your entire life about it, that is how to live a life that glorifies God. When you bring glory to God, He gives you grace for transgenerational impact and influence.

> *When you bring glory to God, He gives you grace for transgenerational impact and influence.*

CHAPTER THREE

TRANSGENERATIONAL Influence and your DOMINION

At the beginning of creation, God said, *"Let us make man in our image, after our likeness: and let them have dominion over the fish of the sea, and over the fowl of the air, and over the cattle, and over all the earth, and over every creeping thing that creepeth upon the earth"* (Genesis 1:26 KJV)

I love how the New International Version puts it, *"Let us make mankind in our image, in our likeness, so that they may rule over the fish in the sea and the birds in the sky, over the livestock and all the wild animals, and over all the creatures that move along the ground."* (Genesis 1:26 NIV)

You will notice in that scripture that God had created other things before God created man. In fact, if we compare that verse with verse 22 of the same chapter, the Bible says *"God blessed them and said, "Be fruitful and increase in number and fill the water in the seas, and let the birds increase on the earth."* One powerful thing I see there is that God created those other things before He created man. How do I know this?

> God created those things for man: God created the fishes of the sea, the birds of the air, and the animals on the land. Those things were resources for man to reign over, have dominion over, and be able to fulfill his mandate.

Man was given a resource that was not given to any other creature: That resource is not your hands because every other creature has hands, that resource is not your head or brain because every other creature has that. That resource was the breath of God. The Bible says, *"And the LORD God formed man of the dust of the ground, and breathed into his nostrils the breath of life; and man became a living soul."* (Genesis 2:7 KJV). The only record of God breathing into anything He created was for man. That, I believe is the greatest resource for dominion. God is clearly saying *"act on my behalf and reign over the earth."* In all of creation, only man was privileged to receive the breath of God.

The Hebrew word for breath is the word *"nashaam"* and it means inspiration. What other blessing does one get from God more than God inspiring you Himself? That means every single one of us has the inspiration of God inside of us. If only we know the meaning of that. It simply means everything God carries, we carry. God is the author of transgenerational influence because He is the God that doesn't have a beginning or an ending. That's why we call Him, the Alpha and Omega. He is the One that knows the beginning and the end. He knows the end even from the beginning. He is the God that began even before the beginning ever began.

> *God is the author of transgenerational influence because He is the God that doesn't have a beginning or an ending.*

That also means that any life that will experience transgenerational influence would be a life that recognizes the breath of God in their inside and is able to leverage the inspiration on their inside. That is because what God did in breathing into man, is giving man His spirit and we know that spirits do not die. The component of man that dies is the flesh but the spirit of man never dies. God gave man a spirit and that is why every other creature dies and perishes completely and every other thing about them dies including the memories of them. But when a man dies, he doesn't actually die but what becomes the death of the influence of man is when that man refuses to leverage the breath of God or the inspiration of God on their inside.

A man that would die and never be remembered is a man that has not learned to leverage the breath of God on their inside. The Spirit of God never dies. The spirit never dies, talk less of the Spirit of God.

Every other mandate which God has given man; to multiply, fill the earth, and have dominion is based on the leverage of the Spirit of God on the inside of a man. A man who will multiply, replenish the earth, subdue it, and have dominion is a man who knows he has the Spirit of God on his inside and leverages that Spirit of God.

That inspiration should not exist inside of one without producing something. The word "inspire" speaks of something that has an antecedence, when you say it inspires something; they have got to be a by-product of inspiration. So, when a man lacks the essence of that inspiration on the inside, we don't witness the byproduct of that inspiration. Many people are walking the surface of the earth who lack the by-product of that inspiration.

> *A man that would die and never be remembered is a man that has not learned to leverage the breath of God on their inside.*

I remember once when I was right in my garage, dancing to some songs on my worship playlist, and all of a sudden I heard the title of a book. This is to explain the inspiration of the Almighty. I thought it was just a title I had to get that day so I wrote it on my whiteboard right in my garage. As I wrote down the title, the next thing I heard were the chapters of the book, they kept on coming and coming and I kept on writing them down until nothing else was coming. That day, I realized that God had just inspired a whole book in a worship session.

A man who learns to work with the inspiration of the Almighty can never lack influence because God will give him ageless truths. God will give you insights that will transcend your lifetime. God will give you truths that will transcend your situation and circumstances. A spirit is not limited by darkness or your upbringing and past. A spirit will hover over darkness and still be able to create light when the time comes. That was exactly what happened in the beginning. The Bible says the earth was covered by darkness and the Spirit of God was hovering over the face of the water.

Darkness cannot stop the Spirit of God from moving. This is what happens when you leverage the Spirit of God on your inside. This inspiration makes us have dominion. Take away the breath of God from any man, take away the inspiration of the Spirit of God from any man, and that man is just like a case without content. That man is now similar to a dog, similar to a pig, and similar to every other thing created.

> **Darkness cannot stop the Spirit of God from moving. This is what happens when you leverage the Spirit of God on your inside.**

Remember where we started from in this chapter, what makes us different is that breath of God on our inside. That breath is the source of our originality, it is the source of our authenticity. Take that away from any man and that man is empty. It is also the source of our rulership. The synonym of the word "dominion" is rulership. That means every man is a king, every man is a king and that is what we are going to talk about in the next session of this book.

The Making of a King: Your Authority and Your Domain

In the last session, we learned how we can leverage the breath of God on our inside. Because that is what makes us have dominion and that is what makes us rule and reign. Every single person that God has created is supposedly a king and two things make a king – territory and authority.

Whenever you see a king, you will always find those two things. A king that doesn't have his territory will never have authority. A king only has authority within his territory. When a king is not where they are supposed to be, they will lack authority. That is why God says in Revelation 5:10, *"And hast made us unto our God kings and priests: and we shall reign on the earth."*
"But you are God's chosen treasure —priests who are kings, a spiritual "nation" set apart as God's devoted ones. He called you out of darkness to experience his marvelous light, and now he claims you as his very own. He did this so that you would broadcast his glorious wonders throughout the world."
1 Peter 2:9 TPT

God wants us to extend his dominion throughout the world. This means that if anyone is going to reign in the domain that God has called them, they must be conversant that they are kings. Kings have a special way of doing things. Kings are royal in the way they do their things: kings talk differently, kings walk differently, kings know that they are leaders in their own right.

That means for you to rule, you need to find your domain. That means you can enjoy and walk in transgenerational influence before you are long dead and gone. It is possible while you are here on earth to still be living a life of transgenerational impact and influence. A king who would live a transgenerational influential life must find his domain.

I always see the world we live in as a puzzle and each piece represents a particular territory on the puzzle board. That means every single piece has a territory on the board. Imagine every individual on the earth being a puzzle piece and the whole world is a puzzle and our territories are marked by the shape of our puzzle piece. Often, I have come to realize as I play with the puzzle with my kids that none of the puzzle pieces are the same. Their shapes and sizes are cut to match the territory that they will sit on. If they are not placed properly, two things happen: they appear out of shape and they leave a void. I am going to write that again for emphasis, when the piece of the puzzle is wrongly placed, they look out of shape and they leave a void.

In other words, almost nothing else can replace a misplaced puzzle piece. You probably would have to sharpen and reshape a particular puzzle piece for it to fit into another place. This is literally what the earth looks like and the way God sees us. All of us are pieces of a puzzle on a jigsaw and we all have our place. If we are out of place, we leave a void. In fact, I believe very strongly that the problem we have in the world right now is that so many people are out of place. That particular problem will continue to exist until those people find their place but our God in His mercy often would have to replace some people. My prayer for you reading this book is that you would not be replaced because our kingship and dominion and living a life of transgenerational impact and influence rest on finding our place.

> **"**
>
> *All of us are pieces of a puzzle on a jigsaw and we all have our place. If we are out of place, we leave a void.*
>
> **"**

I remember an experience I had while I was growing up. We had a neighbor who had a very tough dog, I think it was a German shepherd at that time. But for security reasons, at that time, the dog was always left on the loose and allowed to roam on its own. So, this dog has a special place of his own; you know dogs are territorial. It has its place by the gate of this man's house and the dog was always there. We were living right across the house, and anytime I was sent on an errand by my parents, as I got out of the gate, the dog was always looking fierce and trying to bark at anybody. Going to the front of that gate without having any business there means that the dog would tear you apart. That is because the authority of the dog is within its domain.

I remember vividly that anytime I was sent on an errand, I would have to lean against the wall like some Commando movie to avoid the dog seeing me at all. I would just tiptoe in broad daylight for a few meters and then run but never has this dog ever chased me. Until this particular day, I had tiptoed for a few meters, and all of a sudden I saw this dog on my chase. I bet the adrenaline in me nearly killed me that day. Just looking back and seeing the fierce look of the dog like I am its prey sent me into this realm of Usain Bolt.

I couldn't imagine how my legs could carry me that fast beyond the dog. At a point, I stumbled and I fell. I was expecting the worst to happen only for the dog to continue running beyond me. It was not after me, it was after a herd of sheep. I couldn't believe I just wasted my adrenaline. I was so scared I didn't realize the dog was not after me. I couldn't tell if it started chasing me first and followed the sheep after. But all in all, it proved to me that the dog which had authority in its territory had to show that it had authority in its territory. In the same way, when you find your domain, you have authority in that domain.

In fact, the word kingdom is a combination of the words kingship and domain. So, when you see a king, the king has a kingdom and that means the king has authority in their kingdom which is their domain. For you to have transgenerational impact and influence, you need to know that God has given us a domain to reign in. God has not given any man the authority to reign over another man. The word "leadership" which will be talked about in the next chapter is not reigning over other people, leadership is serving other people. No time in God's agenda has He designed man to reign over man, we are meant to rule over the resources on earth. When we get it right, we see the source of our transgenerational impact and influence.

> **For you to have transgenerational impact and influence, you need to know that God has given us a domain to reign in.**

The Glory of Dominion

Dominion has glory attached to it. If you understand this concept of glory, you will never underestimate yourself or devalue yourself. In fact, it becomes the source of your confidence, esteem, and value for yourself. It is one thing that you are a king but it is another thing for you, as a king, to have glory. As with every domain that God has given you authority over, He also gives you glory in that domain.

Before I move further, I need to define authority. Authority is delegated influence. That means whenever we say someone has authority, they do not have authority by themselves. That authority was designated to them by a higher authority. This is the glory of dominion, which means authority can only be bestowed. Any authority that is not bestowed is illegal.

This is why we have many leaders in our world who are acting under authority that is not bestowed. That is why they act like vagabonds in the place of their authority because it is illegal.

When you see a thief pointing a gun at you and asks you *"your money or your life?"*, you realize that is illegal authority. A legal authority will not tell you *"your money or your life"*, people willingly obey. People are willing to submit to legal authority. An authority that is not legal is by manipulation, legal authority is by motivation. I could write about this over and over again. Legal authority is by inspiration, illegal authority is by intimidation. This is why God doesn't intimidate us into His will or manipulate us into His will because He is trying to show us what legal authority is.

Every one of us must know the difference between these two kinds of authority, so that we do not, at any point in time, make the mistake of doing things that we are not authorized to do. When you are not authorized to do something, you do it out of fear, risk, and intimidation. You do it out of this risk that you might be caught. When it is authorized, you do it out of freedom. That is why you see a policeman stop your car by saying, *"Park"* The policeman is not asking you to park because he has the power to stop your car if you choose not to. He may even be your younger brother. The moment the policeman is in that uniform, he is carrying the authority of the State and country which necessitates you to obey. They have the backing of the government and it is that authority of the government that is asking you to park. If you don't park, you will be in trouble, not with that younger sibling of yours (even though you may be more advanced than him, know more than him, or even have a Ph.D. which he does not have) but with the government that he represents.

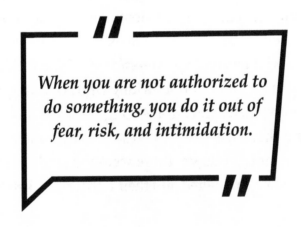

> *When you are not authorized to do something, you do it out of fear, risk, and intimidation.*

The very same way, every human being has authority in their domain, whether their domain is in science, speaking, writing, cooking, hospitality, in sports, entertainment, and whatsoever domain that God has called you into. It is not your influence that you bring in. It is the inspiration of the Almighty, the designated influence of God that you bring in.

That is why the Bible says that *"...whatsoever you bind on earth shall be bound in heaven: and whatsoever you loose on earth shall be loosed in heaven"* (Mathew 16:19). The Bible is referring to the domain that God has given you.

So, if your domain is science, whatever you bind on earth in science shall be bound in heaven. Before the verse quoted above, the Bible says, *"And I will give unto thee the keys of the kingdom ..."* Keys of the kingdom are only released to kings of the kingdom. That is the glory of dominion. The glory of dominion is that you can make things happen. The Greek word for glory is *"doxa"* and it means *"full expression of ''* When a king is basking in his glory, you see a king who is basking in all of his authenticity and aura. A King that lacks authority is a king that lacks glory. In ancient times, when kings could be brought down, those were the kinds of kings that could be conquered and their territories taken from them.

I also want to submit that a king that lacks glory is a king that is out of place. That king will not be able to express himself. I always joke that if the Prime Minister of the United Kingdom comes down to New Zealand where I live, and declares a lockdown, nobody will listen to him. That is because that is not his territory so his authority becomes illegal. He will be sent back to where he came from.

When you are in your domain, you have glory. That glory is not your own, it is from the One who sent you. The source of glory is the grace of God upon our lives, the gifts of God upon our lives that you were given to function in your domain. In the previous chapter, I have explained the dimensions of God on our inside, where I talked about some of the things you can do at the level of GOD. That is the expression of God's grace and glory through you. Whenever you are in your domain, and you do what you have been asked to do based on the authority that has been delegated to you to do it, your impact will undoubtedly last beyond your lifetime. It would be impossible for God's glory not to be seen in you.

> **The source of glory is the grace of God upon our lives, the gifts of God upon our lives that you were given to function in your domain.**

So, if you are reading this book and you don't know how to find your domain, you don't know how to rule and reign in what God has called you to do, I want to admonish that you ask God in prayer, *"Lord, what is my domain? How can I reflect your glory?"* If you know your domain you can ask God, *"What are the graces that you have given me in this area, What is the inspiration that you have given me to function in this area?"*

How Your Dominion Positions You For Transgenerational Influence

All of us have been given different areas of life to rule and reign in. Whenever we are ruling and reigning, we express this uniqueness that nobody else has. When you know this, you don't compete with anybody. I always say that in the kingdom of God there is no competition. Every one of us was made a king and all of us will rule equally. Everybody will rule squarely, you don't need to compete with anybody, you don't need to displace anybody. The problem in our world is that many people do not know that their domain is as attractive as someone they admire.

It doesn't mean dishonoring people, it simply means valuing what you have and loving it enough for you to begin to rule and reign and that glory of God in your domain will begin to express itself later on. Your domain can be uncultivated, some people have been given domains and they have never cultivated it, they have never shown up in their domain and yet they want the authority that belongs to another person's space. In fact, they try to compete in another person's space. I always say that any time you try to compete in another person's space, the best you can be is a photocopy or second class citizen. There are no two kings in one domain. There can only be a real king and a traitor and very soon the traitor will find himself in prison. When you are in the prison of another person's domain you can never find yourself in your own domain.

Don't try to take authority in another person's domain. Find your domain because that is how you have been positioned for transgenerational influence. When you stay in your domain and use your gifts, you bless lives there. There are people called into entertainment, the domain of making movies. There are people called into the domain of science; they just love experimenting and all of the things science entails. There are people called into the domain of aerospace, and they just love it. There are people called into the domain of nature and horticulture and they love it there.

Stay in your domain, some people feel like their domain is not attractive enough and they want to go to another attractive domain. They look at other people's domain and they conclude that they are making money and they want to be there. Some other people see their domain as unpopular so they say, *"I don't have a talent."*

They are renouncing their authority right before their own eyes. If you are reading this book, I submit to you that the very thing that you are commonizing and devaluing, that very thing you think is not attractive to you, is the very source of your authority, the very source of God's glory.

For any of such that you have been given to do, there is the inspiration of God the Almighty, where we started from in this chapter, to back you up. That inspiration is the source of your dominion and authority whether it looks attractive to people or not. If you would dare to enter into that domain, if you would dare to enter into that authority, you will never be forgotten.

I was reading the story of Mary Slessor some time ago. A friend of mine had mentioned her name so I had to go do some research and I realized that this wonderful Scottish woman who was a missionary to Nigeria but with all the glory of the United Kingdom, realized that she was sent not to Lagos, Nigeria a city that is beautiful and urban in every sense. She was not sent to Abuja, she was sent to a place called Calabar and she found her domain there right in the midst of the indigenes and she began to have influence there.

Remember, the inspiration of the Almighty backed her up and this woman ended the killing of twins. She was influential to the end of the killing of twins. She was a foreigner but she learned how to speak Efik, the language of the land. She ended up bringing Christianity into the land and also built several schools. From her story, she was engaged to be married to a man who did not understand the positioning of her authority and she said, *"to hell with this so-called marriage, I am going to my domain"*. Today, we don't know that man, we don't know his name or who he is but we know the name of this woman, Mary Slessor. She lived in her domain, had dominion in the domain, and lived a life of transgenerational impact and influence. Her name will never be erased from the face of the earth.

This reminds me of that woman who poured the oil from the alabaster box and wiped the feet of Jesus with her hair. The disciples and everyone present wondered why someone would waste money like that but Jesus said, *"The poor you will always have among you, but what this woman has done will never be erased from the face of the earth."* That woman exercised an authority that was perhaps the most profound thing she ever did, and that thing is still being talked about today and will still be talked about after we are long dead and gone.

History will never forget people who reigned in their domain, who ruled in their domain, people who exercised the breath of God on their inside and refused to compete with other people in their domain; people who acted on their delegated authority and influence. Because the world never forgets, these are the people who live for transgenerational impact, influence, and dominion.

In the next chapter, we will talk about transgenerational influence and leadership.

> *History will never forget people who reigned in their domain, who ruled in their domain, people who exercised the breath of God on their inside and refused to compete with other people in their domain*

CHAPTER FOUR

TRANSGENERATIONAL Influence and your LEADERSHIP

Leadership is influence. I believe this simple definition summarizes what leadership is all about. It would, therefore, be correct to say that anyone who influences is a leader. I know this may probably sound strange to some people but that is just the simple truth. Many people were brought up to think about leadership in terms of position. Hence, when the word leadership is mentioned, they are forced to think about someone in one exalted position or the other. When you are talking about the concept of leadership, you are referring to the status which comes through a particular result produced by the person considered as a leader.

If we agree that leadership is influence, then it means that anyone who has the ability to influence is qualified to be called a leader or is operating in leadership whether they have a title or not. To influence means to have the power to affect, shape, or regulate other people's behavior by one's actions or inactions. This is the crux of leadership – the ability to have an effect on other people's behavior. The greatest leader of all times, Jesus Christ – our Lord and Savior – revealed this secret to us. Several years after His departure from this world, we still subscribe to His leadership. This is simply because His leadership is still having an effect on us.

It is important to note, before we go deeper into transgenerational influence, that influence could be positive or negative. This means that leadership could be positive or negative. Our emphasis, of course, in this chapter will be on the positive kind of influence, however, I feel it is necessary to underscore the fact that influence can be negative too. What differentiates between a positive and negative influence is the intent or purpose of action and by extension, the result produced after the action.

The interesting thing about influence is that it is not restricted to age, status, color, etc. Though certain people may have a larger scale of influence because of the privileges they have in terms of position or possession but the truth remains that anyone can influence. If you look around you, you will discover that you have been influenced by certain things or people and you have also influenced certain things and people. No one is without some influence. The degree of influence may vary but the ability to influence is a constant for everyone.

> *What differentiates between a positive and negative influence is the intent or purpose of action and by extension, the result produced after the action.*

The Influence Process

To better understand the concept of influence, let's consider what I have tagged as the Influence Process. When we talk about a process, we are referring to the series of actions that take place to achieve the desired result. People who really want to understand certain concepts take the time to study the processes involved. Let's take communication for example. The experts told us that for communication to take place, there must be a message (the information that needs to be passed across), a sender (the person who wants to pass the message), a channel (the medium through which the message will be passed), a receiver (the person who will receive the message from the sender), and then feedback (that proves that the message intended was received and understood as intended). This is a typical communication process (though some other intermediary processes are involved). Similarly, influence also has a process that needs to be understood. When processes are mastered, results are predictable. The influence process involves three main stages as follows:

1. Attraction: This is where every kind of influence begins. You can't be influenced by something that didn't first catch your attention. Attraction is the initiator of influence. We all are attracted to different things or people for different reasons and in different seasons. Some people are attracted to certain kinds of clothes, accessories, cosmetics, etc. either because they have heard so much about them or seen them a lot through adverts. This level of influence is adopted a lot by companies and brands who desire to sell their products. They adopt the power of appeal by bombarding the airwaves with the goodness of their products so as to entice as many people as possible. Influence begins with the ability to capture interest.

2. Retention: At this stage, the attraction is so strong that it has now created an image in the mind. It's like the message has now been encoded. You have seen the picture so much or heard the voice so much that it is now impressed in your mind. The influence has now moved from the outside to the inside waiting for compliance.

3. Compulsion: This is the harvest stage of every influence. It is the action phase where the influence yields fruit. This is the point where the corresponding action of the influence is taken. That's when people buy the product, talk like the person they have been listening to, behave like the person they have been paying attention to. It is often effortless. The action is impulsive because the seed has been sowed and nurtured over time.

This simple process of influence when understood can be used to one's advantage. For instance, many parents want to change their children at the compulsion level when it is a little late. If you understand this process as a leader (parent, pastor, business owner, etc.), you can better influence your followers.

One of our aims for writing this book is to let you see that you need to be deliberate about your influence. That is, who you influence and how you influence. Also, it helps you to be more deliberate about what you allow to influence you. This is what exceptional leaders do. They influence on purpose because they understand that leadership is influence. Now, let's look more closely at who a leader is.

Who Is a Leader?

A leader is someone who has the ability to influence others. This is beyond having a position or title. Once you have the ability to influence at least one person, and that influence goes on to other people in a community, nation, or generation, then you are a leader. A leader is simply someone who leads. Leaders don't lead without doing something. It is their action that inspires others to act.

The fruit of leadership is followership and the root is

influence. Can you picture that for a few seconds? When you see a mango tree, what makes you conclude it is a mango tree? I believe that apart from its unique leaf configuration and orientation, it is the fruits (mangoes) that are visible on the tree that makes the identification of the tree easy. Now, can you imagine a tree called leadership? Just like in the case of the mango tree, the fruits of leadership is followership and the root is influence. This means that followers are proof of leadership which is based on influence. When the leader has a positive influence, the followership will be genuine but when the leader has a negative influence, the followership won't be genuine. Like the scriptures say, "...*A tree is known by its fruits*" (Matthew 12:33). Your ability to grow your influence is the greatness of your leadership.

In different nations of the world, many people think leadership is the position that you hold. Leadership is more than that. Leadership is who you are. That is why some people may be removed from certain positions and still retain their leadership because it is about who they are and it is a function of influence. Moving from one place to another doesn't hinder your ability to lead. Your exit from a position doesn't hinder your ability to influence. You will notice that even when leaders leave a certain position, their followership remains and, in fact, continues to grow because the influence is still there.

This is observable in leaders who move from one nation to another. You will discover that their followers remain faithful to them even though the physical location of their leaders has changed. Thus, the fruit of leadership (followership) always goes with the leader because the root of it is influence. When the root is solid, the fruit continues to grow. This is why certain leaders leave a place and are replaced by another leader but the people continue to follow the leader who has left simply because the root is solid. The fruit of a solid root continues to grow in season and out of season.

There are several things that a leader needs to do to grow influence, but I think the first thing to pay attention to is how that leader got the influence to start with. I believe that a leader must first touch the hearts of the people before he receives the hands of the people. The root must be separated from the fruits. Leadership is beyond the ability to have followers. It is first about influencing people. When people are influenced, they become automatic followers.

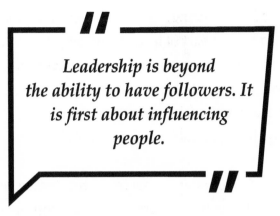

Leadership is beyond the ability to have followers. It is first about influencing people.

The Heart of Leadership

The heart is a very vital organ in the body. It controls the circulation of blood to every other part of the body. A faulty heart automatically means a faulty body. And the body dies the moment the heart stops beating. That is how important the heart is. When we refer to something as the heart of the matter, for instance, we mean that that thing is the central focus or core of the matter. It means every other thing about that matter takes its bearing from that core.

For anything to work effectively, you must understand its core. To get the best out of any gadget or equipment, you need to understand how it operates. Everything that works is built around something that needs to be understood. Leadership is not an exception. To understand how leadership works, and by extension produce the kinds of results that a true leadership should be producing, it is imperative that one understands the heart of leadership. Yes, there is a heart of leadership. Not everyone who is referred to as a leader or put into the position of leadership has the heart of leadership. This reflects in the kinds of results gotten by that leadership at the end of the day.

The heart of leadership is service. A true leader must be willing and ready to serve. I have found myself unconsciously telling people when they commend how great a leader I have been, that it is a privilege to serve them. A leader is truly a servant. Your desire to serve is what positions you to lead. You can never have the heart of a servant and lack the seat of a leader. It always comes. Even when you don't beg or lobby for it, it just finds its way to you. This is because people want a leader that will serve them, not one that will just lord things over them. Leadership is not by force, it is by influence.

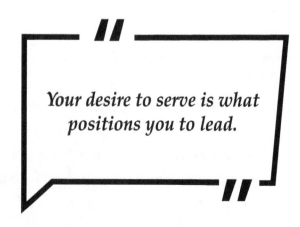

Your desire to serve is what positions you to lead.

Without a sincere desire to serve, even when you are given the opportunity to lead, it will end in failure. The questions a leader should be asking are: How can I be of service to people? How can I be of service to my nation? How can I be of service to my church? How can I be of service to my family? These should be the contemplations of any true leader.

We can also look at the word service as help, so you should be thinking of how you can help as a leader. As a leader, you don't go to be helped, rather you go to help. Looking for where you can help out is what makes people look for you to help them.

Three Levels of Service

We have established that service is what qualifies one for leadership. However, we need to understand that service is in levels. We all are at different levels in life, hence our service is required on different levels. By that, we are talking about the relationship between who serves and who is served.

Whatever level we are in life, it is required that we serve at three levels as follows:

Serving Those Above You

Jesus, the greatest leader of all time, came to do the will of the Father. In other words, Jesus came to serve the Father. He said, *"Not my will, but yours only be done"* He also said, *"If you have seen me, then you have seen the father"* Jesus was completely sold out to represent His Father's interests. In serving the Father, He pointed us to the Father.

Those ahead of us deserve our honor, hence serving those above us begins with honor. Even God said that He will honor those who honor Him (1 Samuel 2:30). The acid test of leadership is serving those above us. When you serve those above you, then you have become a follower. Yes, you are a leader but also a follower.

Honour will give birth to submission. The one you honor, you will submit to. Hence, the language of serving those above us is honor.

> *Honour will give birth to submission. The one you honor, you will submit to.*

2. Serving Those Among You

Jesus also showed us this example. He brought His disciples to His level. He ate with them, drank with them, slept with them, etc. He was among them as one that served. He washed their feet.

One of the things we observe in life is that folks are made leaders among their peers. Everyone can be served but only a few know how to serve. Being served is not leadership but learning to serve is leadership. Learning to position yourself as a tool for help is what makes you a leader. This is how we serve our peers. Thus, the language of serving people among us is being a helpful resource.

3. Serving Those Following You

Before mastering the art of leadership, we must first possess the heart of leadership. Many of the books we read on leadership only show us the art of leadership, however, there is the heart of leadership that we must possess before the art can work effectively.

Learning to serve the people following us will require that we have the right heart; the "I am here to help you" heart. It must be that you believe that you are there to help your generation, community, church, etc. Thus, the language of serving those who follow us is having a heart of humility as it takes humility to serve those we are above.

Traits of a Leader

I believe that certain attributes make for effective leadership. There is a major attribute we will consider – character – which has other traits that an effective leader must have

Character

When it comes to leadership, I believe that people must first be able to connect with your heart, and this will take character. Until people have fallen in love with you, you really can't be said to be a leader over them. One thing that attracts people to a leader, from afar, is character. Character is like a sign which is either saying caution or safety. People can picture us from afar and sense danger or safety. In Matthew 4:19, Jesus simply insinuated that His disciples could feel safe with Him when He said, *"Follow me!"* When a leader uses such a statement, it means he is saying, *"Your life is safe with me, so follow me"* And if we look back, we would realize that Jesus never struggled with anyone that He called. He simply walked up to them to follow Him.

There are many leaders today begging for followers but Jesus never did. The right team members for His team followed Him. They must have seen something in Him that made them follow. Today, He is still calling and multitudes are still following Him. Another example of a safety leader is Elijah (Though he may seem to have been off it because of some of the things he did). When Elisha met him, he immediately followed him. Elisha did not see danger in him, he saw safety.

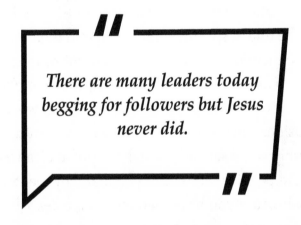

There are many leaders today begging for followers but Jesus never did.

The truth is there are certain character traits people are born with. For instance, from my perspective, I believe Jesus was a calm person. However, Elijah seemed to have been a fiery person. They were two extremes. Thus, there is no one that is exempted from leading because of their character traits; it all begins with the right heart. Elijah was rugged but he had the right heart. Paul was also another example of safety leadership. He said, *"Follow me as I follow Christ."* That is, you can feel safe with me because you know that I follow Christ. Please note that your character may spit danger if you have not proven to be a good follower. Leadership is not about your hostility or gentility but the consistency of your followership. Who have you followed? When people see you, they can tell who you follow.

There was a time I was speaking with some of my team members after service one Sunday, and I was talking about the role of spiritual fathers but told them I wasn't going to mention who mine was, and one of them said, *"We know who He is"* In other words, they simply had seen him in me. When we take care of who we are on the inside, our outside becomes attractive. Your leadership is not safe until you have proven leadership. There are people you see and you that they mentor you simply because you have seen their character. Absalom was an example of a cautionary leader who wanted to dethrone his father. Herod was also another example of a cautionary leader.

Character Traits a Leader Should Possess

Courage
It takes boldness to lead, especially in a crisis. To truly lead in certain seasons of life, you will need to lead not because you lack fear but that you are willing to take the

risk. You need courage. God admonished Joshua to be strong and courageous when it was time to take the mantle of leadership after Moses had died.

The WordWeb Dictionary defines courage as *"A quality of spirit that enables you to face danger or pain without showing fear"* This is such a profound definition of courage. It means you can be courageous even in the face of fear. You may be afraid but you choose to not show the fear by doing what needs to be done. This is a great attribute of leadership.

Often, courage is an essential attribute that sets leaders apart. A good example that comes to mind at this point is the story of David and Goliath.

"Now the Philistines gathered together their armies to battle, and were gathered together at Shochoh, which belongeth to Judah, and pitched between Shochoh and Azekah, in Ephesdammim. And Saul and the men of Israel were gathered together, and pitched by the valley of Elah, and set the battle in array against the Philistines. And the Philistines stood on a mountain on the one side, and Israel stood on a mountain on the other side: and there was a valley between them. And there went out a champion out of the camp of the Philistines, named Goliath, of Gath, whose height was six cubits and a span. And he had an helmet of brass upon his head, and he was armed with a coat of mail; and the weight of the coat was five

thousand shekels of brass. And he had greaves of brass upon his legs, and a target of brass between his shoulders. And the staff of his spear was like a weaver's beam; and his spear's head weighed six hundred shekels of iron: and one bearing a shield went before him.

And he stood and cried unto the armies of Israel, and said unto them, Why are ye come out to set your battle in array? am not I a Philistine, and ye servants to Saul? choose you a man for you, and let him come down to me. If he be able to fight with me, and to kill me, then will we be your servants: but if I prevail against him, and kill him, then shall ye be our servants, and serve us. And the Philistine said, I defy the armies of Israel this day; give me a man, that we may fight together. When Saul and all Israel heard those words of the Philistine, they were dismayed, and greatly afraid."
(1 Samuel 17:1-11)

In the account above, we see that the army of Israel was in trouble. The champion of the Philistine army – Goliath – had come up to dictate the terms of the battle. He offered himself as the decider of the battle's outcome. All the army of Israel needed to do was to choose someone who could fight him. Whoever wins the duel automatically won the battle. However, the Bible says that when Saul and the entire army of Israel heard what the giant had to say, they became terrified. The leader of the army, who should have been a beacon of hope to his men, was afraid. What do you expect the followers to do when the leader is obviously afraid? A whole army became incapacitated because of the threat of one man.

The situation soon became worse. *"And the Philistine drew near morning and evening, and presented himself forty days."* (1 Samuel 17:16). A whole army of strong men became totally demoralized that they couldn't do anything to resist the enemy for forty days. For forty days, morning and evening, they kept listening to Goliath say the same thing he said the first day. Leaders are known to show up strong in the midst of trouble but Saul couldn't do anything in this case.

The young man, David, who had already been anointed as the next king of Israel, in the chapter before this incident, came to check on his brothers (at his father's command) who were part of the army of Israel and it happened that it was the time that the giant came out as usual to say the same thing he had been saying.

"And David left his carriage in the hand of the keeper of the carriage, and ran into the army, and came and saluted his brethren. And as he talked with them, behold, there came up the champion, the Philistine of Gath, Goliath by name, out of the armies of the Philistines, and spake according to the same words: and David heard them. And all the men of Israel, when they saw the man, fled from him, and were sore afraid. And

the men of Israel said, Have ye seen this man that is come up? surely to defy Israel is he come up: and it shall be, that the man who killeth him, the king will enrich him with great riches, and will give him his daughter, and make his father's house free in Israel.

And David spake to the men that stood by him, saying, What shall be done to the man that killeth this Philistine, and taketh away the reproach from Israel? for who is this uncircumcised Philistine, that he should defy the armies of the living God? And the people answered him after this manner, saying, So shall it be done to the man that killeth him. And Eliab his eldest brother heard when he spake unto the men; and Eliab's anger was kindled against David, and he said, Why camest thou down hither? and with whom hast thou left those few sheep in the wilderness? I know thy pride, and the naughtiness of thine heart; for thou art come down that thou mightest see the battle. And David said, What have I now done? Is there not a cause? And he turned from him toward another, and spake after the same manner: and the people answered him again after the former manner. And when the words were heard which David spake, they rehearsed them before Saul: and he sent for him. And David said to Saul, Let no man's heart fail because of him; thy servant will go and fight with this Philistine."
(1 Samuel 17:22-32).

David, who was probably the youngest in that

gathering that day, heard for the first time the same thing the army of Israel had been hearing for days and he couldn't stomach it. One may think that his disposition was different because he was just coming fresh into the camp but that was not the case. The army of Israel, like we already read, became afraid from the first day that Goliath dropped his proposal for the battle. However, in the case of David, a holy anger arose within him. He asked, *"Who is this uncircumcised Philistine that he should defy the armies of the living God?"* David's perspective was different. The army of Israel saw an intimidating giant from the start but David saw an insignificant man who was overstepping his boundaries.

David encouraged Saul and volunteered to go fight the Philistine. In such a seemingly hopeless and fearful situation, David rose to the occasion courageously. He was willing to do what no man in the whole army of Israel could do. By stepping out to face the giant, he showed that he was a leader.

Humility

Jesus showed us how to be humble. God wants us to dress with humility. There are times when courage is needed even if we are humble. Jesus is called the Lion and the Lamb. He was an example of courage and humility. A true leader knows how to be humble and when to be courageous.

"And when the Great Shepherd appears, you will receive a crown of never-ending glory and honor. In the same way, you who are younger must accept the authority of elders. And all of you, dress yourselves in humility as you relate to one another, for 'God opposes the proud but gives grace to the humble.'" 1 Peter 5:4-5 NLT. This scripture establishes the three levels of service we talked about earlier. What stands out the most for me is *"Dress yourselves in humility"* Humility is a character trait that every true leader must possess.

Another word for humility is meekness. According to Wikipedia, "Meekness is an attribute of human nature and behavior that has been defined as an amalgam of righteousness, inner humility, and patience." That means meekness is a blend of other virtues or traits that a good leader should have.

> *A true leader knows how to be humble and when to be courageous*

One man that was described as a meek person in the Bible was Moses. *"Now the man Moses was very meek, above all the men which were upon the face of the earth."* Moses is a classic example of a great leader and the Bible records that he was the meekest man on earth in his generation. No other man was given such a description in the Bible at any time. It takes humility to lead successfully, especially when surrounded by a group of stubborn followers like the Israelites that Moses had to lead.

Humility is a state of the heart that denotes yieldedness to God and deadness to self or ego. By nature, every man is self-seeking. But a humble man has learned to subdue self. You can't be a great leader if you are self-seeking. The opposite of humility is pride (pride can be positive or negative, healthy or unhealthy). This pride I am referring to here is the unhealthy one, such that is self-seeking. It was this pride that led to the expulsion of Lucifer (the devil) from heaven. *"How art thou fallen from heaven, O Lucifer, son of the morning! how art thou cut down to the ground, which didst weaken the nations! For thou hast said in thine heart, I will ascend into heaven, I will exalt my throne above the stars of God: I will sit also upon the mount of the congregation, in the sides of the north: I will ascend above the heights of the clouds; I will be like the most High. Yet thou shalt be brought down to hell, to the sides of the pit."* (Isaiah 14:12-15).

The problem Lucifer had here was that he overestimated himself. He was too self-conceited that he felt he could overthrow God. That is no longer healthy self-esteem. Pride happens when you overestimate your worth and importance so much that you want to put others down as a result. God abhors pride. *"But he giveth more grace. Wherefore he saith, God resisteth the proud, but giveth grace unto the humble."* (James 4:6). God resists the proud as we saw in the case of Lucifer but He gives grace to the humble as we saw in the life of Moses. A leader that would go far must be humble.

> *Pride happens when you overestimate your worth and importance so much that you want to put others down as a result.*

Creativity

Creativity is the bedrock of originality. Since God, our Creator, is creative, a leader also must be creative. God was able to bring the earth we now live in into existence through His creativity. In the same manner, a leader should be able to create possibilities even out of impossibilities seeing that the same creative ability that is in God lies in every man.

It is important to note that the concept of creativity was introduced in the Bible in the midst of chaos:

"In the beginning God created the heaven and the earth. And the earth was without form, and void; and darkness was upon the face of the deep. And the Spirit of God moved upon the face of the waters. And God said, Let there be light: and there was light. And God saw the light, that it was good: and God divided the light from the darkness. And God called the light Day, and the darkness he called Night. And the evening and the morning were the first day. And God said, Let there be a firmament in the midst of the waters, and let it divide the waters from the waters. And God made the firmament, and divided the waters which were under the firmament from the waters which were above the firmament: and it was so. And God called the firmament Heaven. And the evening and the morning were the second day. And God said, Let the waters under the heaven be gathered together unto one place, and let the dry land appear: and it was so. And God called the dry land Earth; and the gathering together of the waters called he Seas: and God saw that it was good.

And God said, Let the earth bring forth grass, the herb

yielding seed, and the fruit tree yielding fruit after his kind, whose seed is in itself, upon the earth: and it was so. And the earth brought forth grass, and herb yielding seed after his kind, and the tree yielding fruit, whose seed was in itself, after his kind: and God saw that it was good.

And the evening and the morning were the third day. And God said, Let there be lights in the firmament of the heaven to divide the day from the night; and let them be for signs, and for seasons, and for days, and years: And let them be for lights in the firmament of the heaven to give light upon the earth: and it was so. And God made two great lights; the greater light to rule the day, and the lesser light to rule the night: he made the stars also. And God set them in the firmament of the heaven to give light upon the earth, And to rule over the day and over the night, and to divide the light from the darkness: and God saw that it was good. And the evening and the morning were the fourth day. And God said, Let the waters bring forth abundantly the moving creature that hath life, and fowl that may fly above the earth in the open firmament of heaven. And God created great whales, and every living creature that moveth, which the waters brought forth abundantly, after their kind, and every winged fowl after his kind: and God saw that it was good.

And God blessed them, saying, Be fruitful, and multiply, and fill the waters in the seas, and let fowl multiply in the earth. And the evening and the morning were the fifth day. And

God said, Let the earth bring forth the living creature after his kind, cattle, and creeping thing, and beast of the earth after his kind: and it was so. And God made the beast of the earth after his kind, and cattle after their kind, and every thing that creepeth upon the earth after his kind: and God saw that it was good. And God said, Let us make man in our image, after our likeness: and let them have dominion over the fish of the sea, and over the fowl of the air, and over the cattle, and over all the earth, and over every creeping thing that creepeth upon the earth. So God created man in his own image, in the image of God created he him; male and female created he them. And God blessed them, and God said unto them, Be fruitful, and multiply, and replenish the earth, and subdue it: and have dominion over the fish of the sea, and over the fowl of the air, and over every living thing that moveth upon the earth.

And God said, Behold, I have given you every herb bearing seed, which is upon the face of all the earth, and every tree, in the which is the fruit of a tree yielding seed; to you it shall be for meat. And to every beast of the earth, and to every fowl of the air, and to every thing that creepeth upon the earth, wherein there is life, I have given every green herb for meat: and it was so. And God saw every thing that he had made, and, behold, it was very good. And the evening and the morning were the sixth day." (Genesis 1:1-31)

This passage explains the concept of creation. This was the beginning of creation and we see God, the Creator of the whole universe, at work here. There is no better way to understand what creation is all about than to study this passage. I would want us to highlight a few things about creation and the nature of a creator from this passage. This will help us to understand the creativity that is expected from a leader. The first thing we notice is that a creator (by extension a creative person) is a problem-solver. From the account above, we saw that God created the heavens and the earth. The first introduction of God is that He is a creator. However, between verses 1 and 2 of Genesis 1, theologians believe that there was a wide gap in time that witnessed the fall of Lucifer as we saw it in the last section. It is believed that it was the arrival of Lucifer and the other fallen angels upon the earth that made the earth void and empty. So, because there was now a problem with the first creative work of God, He had to do something.

One attribute of leaders that makes them outstanding is that they are visionaries. A leader must see within, first, what he desires to see on the outside. That is vision. And vision is critical for creativity. You can't talk about creativity without talking about imagination. A creative person creates with his imagination first. God had a picture of the earth and all that is in it first in His mind before it became a reality physically. This is true for every creator or inventor of our time. It begins in the imagination. All that we now see and enjoy were first created in the imagination before they were produced physically.

The Bible stated that God's Spirit first hovered over the face of the waters. No matter how vast the difficulty before you may be, a leader takes time to brood or meditate over it. Creativity is sparked by meditation. Many people get stuck in the problem because they do not spend enough time in meditation. To unleash your creativity as a leader, you must give time to deep thinking. Deep things come from deep thoughts. A lazy thinker cannot be a creative leader. We can see from the creation story that there is a solution for every problem.

Leaders are bound to encounter problems in their lives and the lives of those who look up to their leadership. Hence, it is important that leaders learn how to unleash their creativity by exerting their minds through thinking. Every major invention that the world has witnessed to date came as a result of someone's critical and deep thinking. God already gave man everything required, in terms of raw materials, to create whatever he needs, he just needs to think and then create.

Finally, on creativity, it is important to stress again that everyone created by God is creative. God passed that ability to every man because the man was made in the image and likeness of God. So, if God is creative, it is only normal to see man expressing creativity too just as we have seen all around us.

Excellence

From the Scriptures, we see how God separated Himself from other gods. All that God made has never needed a review and this communicates excellence. God is the best leader of all. Excellence is a character trait that everyone would love to find in a leader. Excellence is an exceptional approach to an ordinary task. To be excellent simply means to excel at something. It is the ability to stand out in qualities or attributes than others. It means being greater than average. Everyone may be able to get a job done but not everyone can do it excellently. Some people are just so exceptional and flawless in the delivery of their responsibility, craft, work, service, etc.

Such was the case with Daniel and his three friends. *"As for these four children, God gave them knowledge and skill in all learning and wisdom: and Daniel had understanding in all visions and dreams. Now at the end of the days that the king had said he should bring them in, then the prince of the eunuchs brought them in before Nebuchadnezzar. And the king communed with them; and among them all was found none like Daniel, Hananiah,*

Mishael, and Azariah: therefore stood they before the king. And in all matters of wisdom and understanding, that the king enquired of them, he found them ten times better than all the magicians and astrologers that were in all his realm." (Daniel 1:17-20)

Daniel and his three friends were beyond the ordinary. The Bible says that they were ten times better than their colleagues in the university of Babylon. That is excellence. They were outstanding. Their results were way above average. But notice that it was God who gave them the knowledge and skill in all learning and wisdom. Excellence is spiritual. In another place, it was said that Daniel was preferred because he had an excellent spirit. *"Then this Daniel was preferred above the presidents and princes, because an excellent spirit was in him; and the king thought to set him over the whole realm."* (Daniel 6:3). God gives us the grace to excel in whatever we do as His children. The spirit of excellence distinguishes us and sets us apart for the use and glory of God. Let's look at another example to corroborate this.

"And the LORD spake unto Moses, saying, See, I have called by name Bezaleel the son of Uri, the son of Hur, of the tribe of Judah: And I have filled him with the spirit of God, in wisdom, and in understanding, and in knowledge, and in all manner of workmanship, To devise cunning works, to work in

gold, and in silver, and in brass, And in cutting of stones, to set them, and in carving of timber, to work in all manner of workmanship. And I, behold, I have given with him Aholiab, the son of Ahisamach, of the tribe of Dan: and in the hearts of all that are wise hearted I have put wisdom, that they may make all that I have commanded thee;" (Exodus 31:1-6)

In the passage above, we see that God is an excellence-driven God. He had instructed Moses on the specifications needed for the construction of the tabernacle but He didn't stop there. He stated that there were two men, Bezaleel and Aholiab, who had been specially graced to do excellent work in order to achieve the specifications stated earlier. God needed the work to get done excellently, so He put the spirit of excellence into two men specially for the work.

If God loves excellence and goes all the way to deliver it (if you doubt that God is excellent, then look around you right now to the heaven, mountains, vegetations, seas, etc.), then leaders (who are representatives of God on earth) are meant to be excellent at what they do. We already see that excellence works through knowledge, wisdom, and understanding. Then it means that the leader who wants to be excellent in what he does must expose himself to the knowledge, wisdom, and understanding that comes from God. The primary source of these three is God's Word. *"For the LORD giveth wisdom: out of his mouth cometh knowledge and understanding."* (Proverbs 2:6).

> **The leader who wants to be excellent in what he does must expose himself to the knowledge, wisdom, and understanding that comes from God.**

Consistency

Jesus showed us how to be consistent. Being consistent means being in agreement with what is already known. This refers to the ability to reproduce the same result again and again. Jesus was consistent all through His stay on earth and He remains consistent to date. No wonder the scripture has this to say about Him, *"Jesus Christ the same yesterday, and to day, and for ever."* (Hebrews 13:8). Jesus was able to stay true to His course while on earth. He kept teaching and doing things that were consistent with His person and assignment. He was dependable and reliable just like God in whom there is no variableness neither any shadow of turning.

Daniel was a leader who demonstrated consistency. He was a man given to prayer. It was his way of life. He had made a habit out of praying to God daily. He had a time set to meet with God in prayer daily. He wasn't going to trade it for anything even when it was going to cost his life. Let's look at the story;

"It pleased Darius to set over the kingdom an hundred and twenty princes, which should be over the whole kingdom; And over these three presidents; of whom Daniel was first: that the princes might give accounts unto them, and the king should have no damage. Then this Daniel was preferred above the presidents and princes, because an excellent spirit was in him; and the king thought to set him over the whole realm. Then the presidents and princes sought to find occasion against Daniel concerning the kingdom; but they could find none occasion nor fault; forasmuch as he was faithful, neither was there any error or fault found in him.

Then said these men, We shall not find any occasion against this Daniel, except we find it against him concerning the law of his God. Then these presidents and princes assembled together to the king, and said thus unto him, King Darius, live for ever. All the presidents of the kingdom, the governors, and the princes, the counsellors, and the captains, have consulted together to establish a royal statute, and to make a firm decree, that whosoever shall ask a petition of any God or man for thirty days, save of thee, O king, he shall be cast into the den of lions. Now, O king, establish the decree, and sign the writing, that it be not changed, according to the law of the Medes and Persians, which altereth not. Wherefore king Darius signed the writing and the decree. Now when Daniel knew that the writing was signed, he went into his house; and his windows being open in his chamber toward Jerusalem, he kneeled upon his knees three times a day, and prayed, and gave thanks before his God, as he did aforetime. Then these men assembled, and found Daniel praying and making supplication before his God. Then they came near, and spake before the king concerning the king's decree; Hast thou not signed a decree, that every man that shall ask a petition of any God or man within thirty days, save of thee, O king, shall be cast into the den of lions? The king answered and said, The thing is true, according to the law of the Medes and Persians, which altereth not.

Then answered they and said before the king, That Daniel, which is of the children of the captivity of Judah, regardeth not thee, O king, nor the decree that thou hast signed, but maketh his petition three times a day. Then the king, when he heard these words, was sore displeased with himself, and set his heart on Daniel to deliver him: and he laboured till the going down of the sun to deliver him. Then these men assembled unto the king, and said unto the king, Know, O king, that the law of the Medes and Persians is, That no decree nor statute which the king establisheth may be changed. Then the king commanded, and they brought Daniel, and cast him into the *den of lions. Now the king spake and said unto Daniel, Thy God whom thou servest continually, he will deliver thee. And a stone was brought, and laid upon the mouth of the den; and the king sealed it with his own signet, and with the signet of his lords; that the purpose might not be changed concerning Daniel. Then the king went to his palace, and passed the night fasting: neither were instruments of musick brought before him: and his sleep went from him.*

Then the king arose very early in the morning, and went in haste unto the den of lions. And when he came to the den, he cried with a lamentable voice unto Daniel: and the king spake and said to Daniel, O Daniel, servant of the living God, is thy God, whom thou servest continually, able to deliver thee from the lions? Then said Daniel unto the king, O king, live for ever. My God hath sent his angel, and hath shut the lions' mouths, that they have not hurt me: forasmuch as before him innocency was found in me; and also before thee, O king, have I done no hurt. Then was the king exceeding glad for him, and commanded that they should take Daniel up out of the den. So Daniel was taken up out of the den, and no manner of hurt was found upon him, because he believed in his God.

And the king commanded, and they brought those men which had accused Daniel, and they cast them into the den of lions, them, their children, and their wives; and the lions had the mastery of them, and brake all their bones in pieces or ever they came at the bottom of the den. Then king Darius wrote unto all people, nations, and languages, that dwell in all the earth; Peace be multiplied unto you. I make a decree, That in every dominion of my kingdom men tremble and fear before the God of Daniel: for he is the living God, and stedfast for ever, and his kingdom that which shall not be destroyed, and his dominion shall be even unto the end. He delivereth and rescueth, and he worketh signs and wonders in heaven and in earth, who hath delivered Daniel from the power of the lions. So this Daniel prospered in the reign of Darius, and in the reign of Cyrus the Persian." (Daniel 6:1-28)

Daniel was preferred over the other leaders in the kingdom because of the excellent spirit that was found in him (as we saw earlier) and was made the head of all the leaders, as a result. But this didn't go well with these other leaders so they conspired against Daniel by influencing the king to make a decree that will get Daniel into trouble and get him killed in the process. The hearts of men can really be wicked. However, it is interesting to note that the only way they could get Daniel was to use his consistency against him. That is so interesting. They already figured that he was a man of character and integrity and would not put his hand into any kind of evil, so their only option was to convince the king to sign a law that will stop anyone in the kingdom from petitioning any other god or man for 30 days except the king.

They were too sure that Daniel will not bend to that rule and he didn't disappoint them. He was that consistent. His practice was to show up in his room every day, with the windows open, to pray three times. So, immediately after the law was effected, Daniel didn't try to save his face or life. He knew that the law was set in motion to trap him but he wasn't going to trade his consistency for it. He was used to showing up daily before God and no law could stop that, even if it meant death.

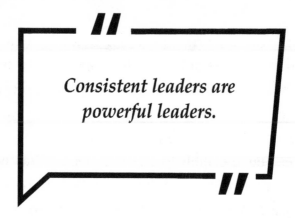

Consistent leaders are powerful leaders.

That is so remarkable. This is how leaders should be with their consistency. Daniel's consistency finally paid off as he was saved from been attacked by lions and because the king, who already preferred Daniel as a leader, witnessed this salvation, he was so excited that he put out a law that everyone throughout the kingdom should worship and fear the God of Daniel. Consistent leaders are powerful leaders.

Progressive

A leader should be progressive, beyond consistency. He should be shining brighter and brighter. Consistency may not be progressive. Hence, it is not enough to be consistent, there should always be something new about us. The best should never be in the past. It is so easy to rest on our oars as leaders. We can easily become complacent if we are not careful. Complacency is the enemy of ascendancy in life. Rick Warren puts it this way, *"The greatest detriment to tomorrow's success is today's success"* Myles Munroe says it like this, *"The greatest enemy of progress is your last success, you could become so proud of what you've already accomplished that you stop moving ahead to what you can still accomplish"*

Complacency is a trap that every leader must avoid. Brian Tracy said, *"Success can lead to complacency, and complacency is the greatest enemy of success."* The lifelong goal of every leader should be how they can get better than yesterday, recording greater success than yesterday's success. Apostle Paul understood this too when he said, *"Brethren, I count not myself to have apprehended: but this one thing I do, forgetting those things which are behind, and reaching forth unto those things which are before, I press toward the mark for the prize of the high calling of God in Christ Jesus."* (Philippians 3:13-14).

There is more ahead that can be achieved than what we have achieved in the past. A progressive leader is one who keeps pressing forward.

Passion

Passion is that zeal, drive, or energy that keeps a leader going. A leader that lacks passion will be stranded at some point. Passion keeps us going when the going gets tough. In the journey of life, we are bound to be faced with trials and challenges. The journey is not always smooth. There are many ups and downs ahead. The leader that will survive the hard times ahead will need some passion. What did you think kept Martin Luther King, Nelson Mandella, etc. going as they pursued their course? It was passion. You cannot have transgenerational influence without passion.

The Psalmist said, *"For the zeal of thine house has eaten me up..."* (Psalms 69:9). Passion is what sets your heart on fire to stay true to the course of leadership. A true leader is passionate. Passion is like the fuel that keeps the fire burning or the car running. Passion keeps the leader going because the journey is far.

The Art of Leadership

According to Wikipedia, art is a diverse range of (and products of) human activities involving creative imagination to express technical proficiency, beauty, emotional power, or conceptual ideas. With this understanding, we can say that the art of leadership is how a leader expresses his leadership prowess. It is how he brings to bear his leadership capabilities. In the end, it is how the leader shows his heart of leadership. That means a leader can have the heart to serve but be deficient in his art of leadership.

The art of leadership talks more about the skills a leader deploys in serving as a leader. It is not enough to know or have something, you must be able to show or serve it to others who need it. This requires work on the part of the leader. A good leader must master the art of leadership because this is the channel through which people perceive his leadership.

Let's take the story of Moses as an example here. Before he encountered God in the wilderness at the burning bush experience, he already had a heart of leadership. He was willing to serve his people. This was why he killed an Egyptian who was oppressing a fellow Israelite. Even though he didn't plan to kill that Egyptian, it happened in the course of fighting for the Israelite in question. This eventually led to Moses' fleeing from Egypt for the fear of the consequence of his action. The king heard about it and was ready to kill Moses (Exodus 2:11-16)

Vital Elements of the Art of Leadership

The art of leadership is a broad topic that should be a book on its own but I will attempt to mention a few elements that help to master the art of leadership.

1. Clarity of Identity: This is where it all begins. A leader must be clear about who he is first of all. You must understand who God has made you before you can understand what He has made you for. This cannot happen without first knowing who God is. God introduced Himself to Moses first. Even though Moses already possessed the heart of leadership, he didn't understand fully that he was a leader God revealed it to him at the burning bush encounter.

2. Clarity of Purpose: Your purpose is God's mandate for your life. It is the essence of leadership. After God revealed to Moses who he had been made, He told Moses about the purpose for which he had been chosen – to go deliver the children of Israel. An understanding of your purpose as a leader is what gives you direction. This is what helps you to know the people you were sent to influence with your leadership.

3. Identifying with the People: You cannot successfully lead a people that you have not identified with. It's not enough to be willing to serve, you must understand the people you have been called to serve. You cannot understand people with who you are not willing to relate. Jesus was able to help humanity because He first identified with humanity. That is why He came in the flesh to start with.

4. Effective Communication: You cannot lead effectively if you can't communicate effectively. Moses had received specific instructions from God about his purpose of delivering the children of Israel. His message was now clear, so he could proceed accordingly. He had something to say to the Israelites and then to Pharaoh, unlike the time when all he could do was fight. People will only accept our leadership and follow us when we communicate clearly what we have to offer. Leadership cannot succeed without communication.

5. Motivating the People: People don't always feel like going forward. We see that clearly in the journey of the children of Israel towards the promised Land. Many times, they felt like going back to their comfort zone – Egypt. They didn't mind the accompanying hardship. Moses stepped in many times to motivate them. A true leader must master the skill of motivation. This may come with some negotiation per time too. To get to the goal or achieve the vision, people need motivation and leaders must be able to give that.

The Principle of Personal Growth

I believe strongly that no organization grows a leader, it takes personal development to grow. Positions don't grow leaders, responsibilities do. There must be consistency of personal growth. Responsibility is the key to personal growth.

A true leader never stays the same. A true leader is always desirous of a new level. If people are depending on you for their growth, then you have got to be learning, and improving yourself. You can't be telling your followers the same thing every time they contact or interact with you.

> **A true leader never stays the same. A true leader is always desirous of a new level.**

A leader cannot afford to be on the same level. Your influence as a leader is tied to your growth. To be more influential, you have to be more and do more. This is a call to responsibility. My father, Bishop Oyedepo, was once asked how he is able to stay alert to do the kind of work that he does. They wanted to know if he takes coffee or some other kind of stimulants to stay active but he said the secret is responsibility. That is what keeps him alert. When you have a generation that you are responsible for, you cannot afford not to be alert and growing.

The reason why some people are not growing is simply that they lack a sense of responsibility. In our commission, we have 12 pillars which we run through every year. That means we go over each pillar every month. For instance, at the time of writing this book, we are considering prosperity. A person who has been part of the church for 3 years will already have the guidelines we use and an idea of each pillar. However, it will be irresponsible of me to show up the same every time I have to teach on each subject. The responsibility lays a demand on me to grow; so that I come with fresh insights every time even though I am teaching on the same subject.

Personal growth is important in leadership. Paul said "necessity is laid upon me" He meant that responsibility was beckoning him. A responsible leader is a growing leader. He ensures that he is doing all that is possible to become better in all realms of human existence: spirit, soul, and body.

We talked about avoiding the trap of complacency as a leader under the character traits of a leader. A leader who would be progressive is committed to personal growth or development. The leader, just like anyone who expends himself, is prone to depletion. The law of diminishing returns is real in the life of the leader too. Diminishing returns is a term in economics. Oxford Languages Dictionary defines it as *proportionally smaller profits or benefits derived from something as more money or energy is invested in it.* In the long run, the level of investment in your personal growth that brought you to where you are at the moment would no longer be able to achieve the kind of results that you desire as a leader. You must scale up.

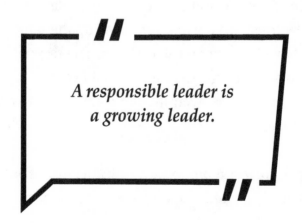

A responsible leader is a growing leader.

The result a leader gets is only as good as the investment the leader makes in himself. You can't give what you don't have and as you give what you have, you must increase what you have. Leadership is draining because you are always giving as a leader. We have established earlier that a leader is more concerned about helping and not been helped. Hence, the leader must always put himself in a position where he can help. The only help a leader must seek is that which helps him to become better as a person.

How Personal Growth Positions a Leader for Transgenerational Influence

The art and heart of leadership positions a leader for transgenerational influence. Jesus is still leading now even though He is no longer with us physically today. We also have patriarchs of faith who have gone home to be with the Lord but are still leading today.

I was listening to some late Dr. Myles Munroe's messages recently and he was teaching me certain deep things about prayer. What he said changed my prayer life. In other words, he is still leading even though he has gone home to be with the Lord.

Some people refer to me as their leader today but I have

never met them while I was pastoring in the church where I had pastored before. Some were not even in that church when I was a pastor there. They joined the church after I left but they still subscribed to my leadership because of what they met - the influence.

You may castigate a leader but you can't erase his influence. True influence cannot be erased. The art and heart of leadership will help you lead beyond your lifetime. Personal growth puts a leader in a position where his leadership is more effective and relevant because the better the leader, the better and more long-lasting his influence.

We already know that God cannot bless generations without a man or woman that would serve as the instrument He will use. That is why God is always seeking men that He can use. He looks for available men who will be willing to go all the way. God needed a man that would sustain the lineage of men when He was set to destroy the earth with a flood, and He found Noah and his family. As evil as men of that age had become, He found a man who was positioned for transgenerational influence. *"And the LORD said unto Noah, Come thou and all thy house into the ark; for thee have I seen righteous before me in this generation."* (Genesis 7:1).

God needed a man in that generation and Noah was found worthy because he distinguished himself through personal growth. It takes a man that is growing personally to be found righteous in the midst of a wicked generation. That is a man who has taken the responsibility to be different. This is the man God is looking for in every generation. When you take your personal growth seriously, you position yourself for transgenerational influence.

> *"*
>
> *When you take your personal growth seriously, you position yourself for transgenerational influence.*
>
> *"*

CHAPTER FIVE

TRANSGENERATIONAL
Influence and
the KINGDOM
OF GOD

The kingdom of God refers to God's government. Jesus was teaching His disciples to pray when he revealed something about God's kingdom, *"Thy Kingdom come. Thy will be done in earth, as it is in heaven."* (Matthew 6:10 KJV). Every kingdom has its influence. A kingdom cannot exert dominion outside its sphere of influence. A king is the highest authority in a kingdom, hence the symbol of the influence of that kingdom. When a king shows up, he represents the kingdom. That is why whatever the king says is binding on his kingdom. *"Where the word of a king is, there is power: and who may say unto him, What doest thou?"* (Ecclesiastes 8:4)

God's kingdom refers to God's way of doing things. It tells us about His constitution and thoughts. In Isaiah 55:8, we see that God's thoughts and way of doing things are different from ours. It behooves us, therefore, to understand God's way of thinking and doing things. Because to extend the influence of God to the earth like it is in heaven, then we must understand the will of our King. We must understand what He wants and how He wants it done.

We are ambassadors of God's kingdom here on earth (2 Corinthians 5:20). What ambassadors do is working for the benefit of the kingdom they represent. They are always looking for ways they can ensure that the influence of their kingdom is strengthened and sustained.

Jesus came to embody the kingdom of God here on earth. He introduced us to God, His thoughts, and His ways. This was what His ministry on earth was all about. He unveiled certain dimensions of God's operation that were strange to many people in His days. Indeed, God's government was upon His shoulders, *"For unto us a child is born, unto us a son is given: and the government shall be upon his shoulder..."* (Isaiah 9:6a)

The religious leaders particularly had a very hard time understanding Jesus and what He represented. He disrupted their thinking and way of doing things by God's way of thinking and doing things. Many times, He let the people see that whatever they saw Him do was what the Father would have Him do. He stressed that He and the Father were one. This is how a true leader who will have transgenerational influence must conduct himself – thinking and doing things the way God does.

Every kingdom operates by a constitution that dictates the actions allowed or disallowed in that kingdom. God's thoughts, and by extension His way of doing things, are revealed by His Word. Hence, to understand God's kingdom, you must be conversant with His Word. God's Word is God's constitution. God's Word is

God's influence.

"And the seventh angel sounded; and there were great voices in heaven, saying, The kingdoms of this world are become the kingdoms of our Lord, and of his Christ; and he shall reign for ever and ever." (Revelations 11:15)

"For unto us a child is born, unto us a son is given: and the government shall be upon his shoulder..." (Isaiah 9:6a). What God expects from us as leaders, who represent His interests, is for us to ensure that the kingdoms of the world become the kingdoms of our Lord. We are meant to use our influences here on earth to push His influence. Wherever we find ourselves in the institutions of the world, God has placed us there to assert the influence of His kingdom. This is our highest calling. This is the whole essence of mastering the art and heart of leadership. This is the whole essence of transgenerational influence.

> **Wherever we find ourselves in the institutions of the world, God has placed us there to assert the influence of His kingdom.**

God's Original Plan for The Earth

I believe God's original plan for the earth was for man to extend His kingdom to the earth as revealed in Genesis 1:28,

"And God blessed them, and God said unto them, Be fruitful, and multiply, and replenish the earth, and subdue it: and have dominion over the fish of the sea, and over the fowl of the air, and over every living thing that moveth upon the earth." (KJV)

Jesus came to establish God's kingdom, government, and His culture on the earth. He showed man how to fulfill that divine plan. The reason why we have healings on earth is that there is no sickness in heaven. This was why Jesus went about healing people when He was here on earth.

The reason why we preach prosperity on earth is that there is prosperity in heaven. The reason why we preach breakthrough on earth is that there is no breakdown in heaven. There is no failure in heaven and God expects us to succeed on earth because we are meant to experience heaven on earth. The idea is to extend the influence of heaven to the earth.

In other words, whatever is not permitted in heaven is not expected to be permitted on earth. We are meant to bring down God's government here on earth. We cannot talk about the kingdom of God without talking about the Church of God. And I believe that is one of the reasons why God instituted the church. What we do when we preach is to explain God's constitution so that everyone is conversant with it. When we align with God's constitution, then we are accepting the government of Christ, submitting to His rulership, and of the increase of His government, there shall be no end.

Life's Greatest Pursuit And Priority

"Seek the Kingdom of God above all else, and live righteously, and he will give you everything you need" (Matthew 6:33 NLT). Since we have considered earlier that God's original design is that His kingdom is established upon the earth, then man's greatest pursuit should be the establishment of that kingdom. We should be running towards the establishment of that kingdom. For those who push the kingdom of God, the kingdom of God pulls them forward. It begins with you initiating the push. Those who are willing to die for the kingdom, the kingdom ensures that they live.

God's original plan is to extend His kingdom on earth,

our greatest pursuit should be establishing that kingdom. There are two aspects of this establishment:

Expanding God's Kingdom: Here, the concern is to make Jesus famous. If as a leader I have character traits that can attract people to me, then I should use it as a tool to make Jesus famous. We expand the kingdom by expanding its influence.

Enlarging God's Kingdom: This is about increasing the capacity of the kingdom. We can make more room available for God's kingdom through our gifts, talents, resources, etc. Some of us are gifted for the marketplace, politics, etc. As we exert dominion in these spheres, we increase the capacity of God's kingdom.

If a man pursues the kingdom of God by expanding its influence and enlarging its capacity, without a doubt, that man's influence will never end too. This is because God's kingdom can never end. *"Thy throne, O God, is for ever and ever: the sceptre of thy kingdom is a right sceptre."* (Psalms 45:6) *"Thy kingdom is an everlasting kingdom, and thy dominion endureth throughout all generations."* (Psalms 145:13). God's dominion here on earth will transcend generations. He only seeks men who will partner with Him to ensure this continuity through transgenerational influence.

CHAPTER SIX

TRANSGENERATIONAL
Influence and
VISION

Vision is a picture of the future. As a leader, what have you pictured about the future of those you are leading? Transgenerational influence cannot be separated from vision. There has to be a vision that is so strong before a leader can influence generations after him.

God told Abraham that he will be given possession as far as his eyes can see. Today, we are still beneficiaries of the blessings of Abraham several years after he has gone. I know people who have been called true sons of Kenneth Hagin. He is still birthing sons, even today, because of his influence. David went a long time ago but Jesus is still referred to as the son of David.

Vision is so powerful because it can help you lead a generation towards a future that you have seen even when you have no direct contact with that generation. God has seen our future even when we are not yet there, *"For I know the thoughts that I think toward you, saith the LORD, thoughts of peace, and not of evil, to give you an expected end."* Jeremiah 29:11 KJV

It is not enough for the leader to have a vision for his people, he must also know the direction through which they will get to that destination. There are visionary leaders but people will appreciate practical leaders more. Practical leaders have an edge because they know how to take their people to the great future they have seen.

Jesus exemplified this by raising 12 disciples. He already knew what was ahead. He had seen the future but He figured that He had too little time. Hence, He poured Himself into 12 men first. He transferred that same vision into them so that they were empowered to retain the influence cycle that we still enjoy today. Leaders should learn not only how to picture the future but how to get their people there. A true leader should raise other leaders.

> **It is not enough for the leader to have a vision for his people, he must also know the direction through which they will get to that destination.**

The Invisible Realm Where Champions Dwell

It was John Maxwell who said that *"True leaders see more than others, and see before others"* Thus, the realm of champions is the realm of seeing more and seeing before. Seeing more can be termed foresight while seeing before can be termed far sight.

Before Covid-19 came, as a church, we already started seeing that there were things that needed to be changed in our system and we began to immediately implement that about one year before the pandemic. So, as a church, we were not hit by the crisis that came with the pandemic like many other churches were.

One of the greatest undoings of a leader will be procrastination. As a leader, it is not enough to see before, you must also act fast. Execution must be prompt. Abraham showed us how to act fast. When he was asked to leave his father's land, he acted fast. Also, when God asked him to sacrifice his only son – Isaac – he acted fast.

According to Oral Roberts, *"being able to see what others have not seen will be able to help you do what others have not seen."* This is one thing that can separate you from the pack. As leaders, we should be able to see before others and see ahead of others. Jesus saw many things ahead and pre-informed His disciples ahead to prepare their minds.

Evolution of Vision

Visions don't change but they can expand. I have seen people who try to take me back memory lane to days when I said the vision I saw was serving as a pastor in ministry all life long, and a few of them feel that this has changed because I now operate more as a life coach. The truth is that I am still a pastor and that will never change, the vision has only evolved to find expression in some other ways.

How you know that your vision has not changed is that you still do the same things you usually do, only that the expressions may change. New phases of your vision will emerge and you need to be comfortable with that, even though people may criticize you.

Vision expands. It can be magnified that you begin to see aspects of the same vision that you never saw before and you begin to take steps that you never thought about before. No God-given vision is cast in stone. Most times, we can only see a fraction of what God will do through us or where He is taking us to. Apostle Paul explained this when he said, *"For we know in part and prophesy in part"* (1 Corinthians 13:9 NKJV). As long as we are on this side of eternity, we shall always see and prophesy in part. Only God sees the whole picture.

The way it works is this, as we move closer to the fulfillment of the vision that we have seen through execution, we see more aspects that were not obvious before. The more we see, the more we are able to say. This means your vision expansion is directly proportional to your evolution. The more you grow in your knowledge of God and walk with Him, the clearer the vision becomes to you.

> **The more you grow in your knowledge of God and walk with Him, the clearer the vision becomes to you.**

Therefore, you need to be comfortable with being misunderstood or criticized because of your vision evolution. As you evolve, you become a mystery that many want to unfold. This is because people want to find a definition for everything or be able to explain everything but it doesn't work that way when you are walking with God. Many things will be unexplainable.

It is important that you are faithful to the vision God has shown you. *"Whereupon, O king Agrippa, I was not disobedient unto the heavenly vision:"* (Acts 26:19). Apostle

Paul was on trial here before one of the greatest kings of his time. He needed to plead his case but didn't fail to explain that he was operating based on a compelling vision. He narrated how Jesus had appeared to him and given him a mandate. This was a kingdom matter. It was about enforcing God's influence upon the earth and Paul was ready to go all the way to see that vision adhered to.

God understands the power of a compelling vision in ensuring the expanding and enlarging of His kingdom on earth. It takes a compelling vision to go all the way. God will continually impress pictures of the future in our hearts as leaders to ensure the propagation of His kingdom. We will need to be obedient to these visions in our heart per time if we must partake in transgenerational influence.

LAST WORDS

In the last six chapters, we have explained what transgenerational influence is all about. Using practical examples from the Bible, our own experiences, and that of others, we believe that we have helped to create the hunger in you to not just live but live with generations to come in mind.

God didn't send you here on earth to just come and enjoy yourself and leave without any influence that transcends generation. You are a part of a big puzzle and you need to understand that if you don't fit in well, by showing up and delivering all that has been deposited in you, certain people will not fit in well.

Imagine if Jesus did not die on the cross to restore men to God. Imagine if Abraham did not choose to walk with God. Imagine if all the books, messages, etc. that have blessed you thus far and have kept you living a fulfilled life were not written or preached.

Life becomes more beautiful as we all play our parts. We cannot afford to live without leaving something worthwhile and remarkable for the generations coming after us. Generations to come should be able to give thanks to God because of the rich inheritance that we will leave behind for them.

We hope that through reading this book, you have been inspired to see beyond you and now. We look forward to your transgenerational testimonies.